HOW TO WRITE GOOD ESSAYS AND CRITICAL REVIEWS

COLES EDITORIAL BOARD

Bound to stay open

Publisher's Note

Otabind (Ota-bind). This book has been bound using the patented Otabind process. You can open this book at any page, gently run your finger down the spine, and the pages will lie flat.

ABOUT COLES NOTES

COLES NOTES have been an indispensible aid to students on five continents since 1948.

COLES NOTES are available for a wide range of individual literary works. Clear, concise explanations and insights are provided along with interesting interpretations and evaluations.

Proper use of COLES NOTES will allow the student to pay greater attention to lectures and spend less time taking notes. This will result in a broader understanding of the work being studied and will free the student for increased participation in discussions.

COLES NOTES are an invaluable aid for review and exam preparation as well as an invitation to explore different interpretive paths.

COLES NOTES are written by experts in their fields. It should be noted that any literary judgement expressed herein is just that – the judgement of one school of thought. Interpretations that diverge from, or totally disagree with any criticism may be equally valid.

COLES NOTES are designed to supplement the text and are not intended as a substitute for reading the text itself. Use of the NOTES will serve not only to clarify the work being studied, but should enhance the readers enjoyment of the topic.

ISBN 0-7740-3433-5

© COPYRIGHT 1998 AND PUBLISHED BY
COLES PUBLISHING COMPANY
TORONTO - CANADA
PRINTED IN CANADA

Manufactured by Webcom Limited
Cover finish: Webcom's Exclusive **DURACOAT**

CONTENTS

INTRODUCTION

As our title suggests, this booklet is designed to give you — the student writer — some insight into the many factors that your teacher takes into consideration when grading your essays.

In the pages which follow, you will find examples of various types of essays written by your contemporaries. The first theme in each section is, in general, the poorest of the series; the last, the best. The introductions and commentaries which discuss the essays should lead you to an awareness of their merits and defects; the exercises which follow each set of essays will give you practice in transforming poor or fairly good essays into "A" papers.

Thoughtful consideration of the mistakes of other students will, we feel, help you learn to avoid their blunders in your own writing. On the other hand, seeing how students have successfully solved awkward writing problems which you yourself often face should provide you with some useful suggestions for your own future essays.

Achieving higher grades on your school papers is not, of course, an end in itself. Your writing assignments are planned by your teacher to prepare you for your role in the adult world. All of our arts, sciences, and inventions depend upon man's ability to communicate his thoughts to his neighbours and to future generations. Writing is thus the means by which man has achieved pre-eminence among all living things.

WHAT IS AN ESSAY?

A recent university survey has revealed that a remarkably high percentage of high school graduates who have been writing essays for years had only the vaguest possible notion of precisely what an essay was. In general, they tended to define any series of related sentences on the same subject as an essay.

More remarkable was the discovery that many were unconcerned by the fact that they could see no correlation between the amount of work they put in on an essay and the grade it received. They conceived of the relative success or failure of a paper as a *mysterious occurrence* over which they had no control. Some essays "came off," they felt, while others were "just no good" in spite of their efforts.

Such ideas, of course, are far from the truth. Successful essay writing is neither a gift of the gods nor the result of luck; rather, it is the almost inevitable product of applying a reasonable amount of effort to the assignment at hand. The *trick* — if there is any — is in learning to apply your efforts in the proper direction.

An essay stripped to its basic skeleton is a collection of words. But what are words? Or, more precisely, why do we use words? The answer is obvious: to communicate our thoughts to others. And why do we communicate? Think about it, and you'll agree that every communication, whether spoken or written, is designed to elicit some response from or to have some effect on your audience.

This, too, is the function of an essay. It is a way of communicating with an audience for the purpose of affecting it in some way. Depending upon the reason for which a successful essay was written, its readers may respond by agreeing with the ideas of the writer, or by being led to a new understanding of the facts he presents, or perhaps by being forced to admit that other points of view from those they held before reading the essay must be considered.

Thus we have arrived at a definition of an essay: a piece of writing designed to affect its readers in a manner determined by its author. Keep this definition in mind as you read the essays in this booklet. You will find the best essays tend to sway you towards the author's position on his subject, whereas the worst will do no more than bore you. And — most important — keep the definition in mind as you begin to write your own next essay!

PREPARATIONS FOR WRITING

No one — no matter what he is attempting — can hope to accomplish anything worthwhile unless he knows what he wishes to accomplish before he begins work. If you expect to produce a successful essay, before you begin writing you must decide upon the effect you want your essay to have on your readers.

The following preparations — time-consuming as they may be — are the essential first steps in writing a good essay. You will only weaken your chances of producing a successful essay if you begin writing before you are ready.

Until you have clearly defined your own attitudes towards the subject of your paper, you are in no position to think of influencing others. Honesty at this stage is vital. In many cases, after thinking about the subject you have been assigned, you will find that you simply do not know enough about it to formulate an opinion.

If you find yourself in such a position, you must, of course, obtain more information. Consider filling in your background by consulting an encyclopedia or some other reference book in your school library. If such aids are for some reason unsatisfactory, the person to consult is your teacher.

Once you have clarified your own thinking on the subject, you are ready to begin outlining the methods you will use to bring your readers to your point of view. Always be aware of the possibility that the logic which led you to your conclusions may *not* be the most effective way of winning others to your position. For example, you may hate war because it is denounced in the Bible and because a close friend of your family has been killed in battle. Non-religious readers who have never been acquainted with combat soldiers may pay little attention to an essay presenting only these reasons for abolishing warfare.

Thus, when searching for material to support your opinions, think in terms of convincing your readers rather than of showing why you, personally, feel as you do. The more objective the facts and the more universal the examples you present, the more meaningful and effective your essay will be.

After deciding how you wish to affect your readers and selecting the facts and examples which will accomplish this most effectively, you are ready to organize your material into the most forceful presentation possible. Various types of organization will be discussed in Chapters 1 through 7 of this book.

THE ELEMENTS OF AN ESSAY

Now you are ready to begin writing your essay. Let's see what is required to assure you of an "A" grade on it. Although the best writing is not produced by too close an adherence to a strict formula, it is always wisest to follow the basic "rules-of-thumb" unless you have good reasons for deviating from them.

In general, the first and last sentences in an essay are the most important and should receive your most careful attention. The first words that strike a reader's eye will either interest him in what you have to say or convince him that reading your essay is not worth his trouble. Your concluding remarks, on the other hand, are those he will remember most vividly after finishing the essay.

Introductions can be handled in any number of ways, and the most original opening is often the most effective. Your opening lines, however, do have some definite functions to perform: in addition to commanding the reader's attention, they should interest him in your subject, imply your attitude towards the material, and, in some cases, suggest the procedure you will follow in dealing with your subject.

No matter how you begin your essay, however, there is one rule which must never be broken. You must always keep your bargain with your readers. If you ask a question in the introduction, you must either answer it or show why it is unanswerable in the body of your paper. If you attract attention with an anecdote, you must prove the aptness of your story to the essay. If you begin by stating your opinion, you must show readers either why your thoughts should interest them, or why they should agree with you.

The conclusion to an essay offers fewer opportunities for originality. Your summary statements must follow logically — almost inevitably — from the material which precedes them. It is often most effective to be as concise as possible, for a few well-chosen and neatly phrased words are more easily remembered than long, discursive sentences.

Long essays that are primarily concerned with the presentation of facts are often best ended with summaries which remind the readers of what has been said earlier. Short essays, however, do not require summary statements for, since the readers will have no trouble in retaining all your material in mind until they finish the essay, a summation would be repetitious.

Long or short, however, remember that the purpose of every essay is to affect a reader in some way. If you feel he should act on your suggestions, tell him so. If you wish him to recognize the importance of what you have written, emphasize its possible consequences for him. If you think that, in spite of your presentation, he is likely to disagree with your conclusions, you might wish to end your essay by stressing the validity of your opinions.

Rhetorically, your final paragraph will have the function of unifying your essay. For this reason it is often effective to repeat a key word or phrase from your introductory remarks.

The central section, or body, of an essay is impossible to discuss in any detail without reference to the different "types" of essays. Problems of organization, development, focus, and the like will be considered in the introductions to the later sections of this book. Certain considerations which apply to all types of essays are of interest here, however.

While everyone *is* entitled to his opinion on any subject, no one can expect to convince his neighbour — or anyone else — of the validity of his ideas unless he reveals in some detail his reasons for feeling as he does. Since the purpose of writing is, by definition, to convince the reader of the "rightness" of your assertions, backing up what you say is even more important in an essay than in oral communication.

Thus every statement you make in an essay must be supported by evidence which the reader will accept. You must offer him whichever facts, examples, and illustrations are required to lead him to your position on your subject.

Any generalization, until proved otherwise in the context of an essay, is meaningless. For example, were you to say — without further qualification — that college graduates earn more money than non-graduates, you would be quite wrong although the statement appears true on the surface. To prove you false, your reader would only have to recall that many plumbers, electricians, construction workers and the like make higher wages than some college-trained school teachers. And, whether your unsupported assertion be a major point in your essay or an almost irrelevant sidelight, his awareness of your careless thinking will prejudice him against everything else you have to say.

STYLISTIC CONSIDERATIONS

As the several chapters of this book will illustrate, an author's purpose in writing determines the organizational pattern his essay will follow, and the choice is wide. The same stylistic considerations, however, must be observed for all varieties of essays.

A totally successful essay must be perfect mechanically and grammatically. A writer who betrays his ignorance of the basic usages of the English language will never — no matter how thought-provoking his ideas — command the respect of an educated audience. An "A" grade indicates that an author has turned in a nearly flawless, mechanical performance.

In addition, every essay you write must say something worth saying. A teacher who gave a high grade to a technically flawless essay which was simple-minded in content would be insulting the intelligence of all other students in his class.

The tone of your essay should always suit the subject under discussion. An essay which dealt with inherently serious material — such as the assassination of President Kennedy or the effects of polio on children — in a lighthearted or comic manner would offend every reader. Conversely, pleasant subjects — your vacation trip or a child's first Christmas (unless, of course, they ended in tragedy) — should not be treated in the style of scientific textbooks.

Finally, and perhaps most important, try to handle every writing assignment in a relatively original way. Do not follow the same format for every essay you write: You will never fully realize your own potential unless you experiment with new forms and techniques. Top grades, you will find, invariably go to those essays which, while paying attention to the fundamental rules of essay writing, interpret these rules in fresh and exciting ways.

WHAT TEACHERS LOOK FOR IN GRADING

Your teachers want you to succeed. It is their job to help you to learn to use your abilities so that you can succeed. To supply that help, they need to be both encouraging and critical, like the golf instructor who says, "That drive was better. Now let's have a little more follow-through on the next one. And keep your eye on the ball!"

Usually your teachers will try to find one or two features of your writing that they can honestly praise. (They will often, in fact, be much kinder in evaluating your writing than we have been in discussing the anonymous essays in this book.) But along with their praise, your teachers will generally offer suggestions for improvement. These may involve only minor points, or they may cause you to look anew at your subject in order to improve its content or organization. Sometimes, to comply with the suggestions, you may need to rewrite.

Most teachers take into consideration all the following items:

	Good	Fair	Poor
Quality of content	——	——	——
Originality of treatment	——	——	——
Unity (sticking to the subject)	——	——	——
Coherence (arrangement of parts)	——	——	——
Emphasis	——	——	——
Paragraphing	——	——	——
Diction	——	——	——
Grammatical usage	——	——	——
Sentence structure	——	——	——
Spelling	——	——	——
Punctuation	——	——	——

An excellent composition would have most of the check marks in the good column; it would certainly be *good* in content, unity, and coherence, and in some of the others, and probably no worse than *fair* in any category. A fair composition would no doubt be checked *good* for two or three of the items, *poor* for two or three, and *fair* for the rest. A poor composition would have most checks in the *poor* column, though several might appear in the *fair* or even the *good* column.

Some examiners check points on rating scales similar to the following:

Contents and Organization

Convincing	———————	Unconvincing
Organized	———————	Unorganized
Thoughtful	———————	Superficial
Broad	———————	Limited
Specific	———————	Vague

Style

Fluent	———————	Stilted
Cultivated	———————	Vulgar
Strong	———————	Weak

Usage

Correct writing forms	———————	Incorrect writing forms
Conventional grammar	———————	Substandard grammar

Notice that teachers who follow a similar plan give fifty per cent of a grade for content and organization and the other fifty per cent for style and usage. Probably most teachers attempt to preserve approximately such a balance.

Your own teachers no doubt use some variation of one of the two grading systems shown, though their check lists may be only in their heads rather than on paper. They may, for their own reasons, choose to put special emphasis on two or three of the characteristics of good writing. Unquestionably, though, they will stress both *what you say* and *how you say it*. The truly excellent theme is excellent in both of these respects.

FORM AND CONTENTS OF THIS BOOK

The first two chapters of this book deal primarily with the restrictions as well as the obligations imposed upon you by the nature of the two different types of essay assignments. Later chapters deal with specific types of essays.

When your teacher asks you to write an essay at home, he expects you to approach the assignment in a somewhat different manner from the way you would handle an "impromptu." Therefore, the first two chapters deal with the "at home" essay and the impromptu. The remaining chapters concern five types of essays that may be written either at home or in class.

The first two chapters should be studied in conjunction with the five units which follow them, for you may be asked to write various types of essays under both conditions. An "at home" essay by definition differs in certain respects from an "in class" essay of the same type, but, on the other hand, both have a great deal in common. It will be up to you to utilize whichever suggestions you find appropriate to specific assignments.

Obviously, we have not been able to discuss all the different types of essays in a book of this size. We think you will find, however, that the varieties considered are the types you most often will be asked to write.

Also, keep in mind that what is said of one type of essay will, frequently, apply equally well to other types. We have avoided duplication of commentary wherever possible, for we assume that you will borrow whatever techniques and suggestions suit your purposes for writing any and every type of essay.

CHAPTER 1

THE "AT HOME" ESSAY ASSIGNMENT

Often when your teacher assigns an out-of-class essay he will present you with a rather broad topic and permit you to develop it in any way, and from any point of view, you wish. Such is the type of essay assignment we shall consider in this chapter.

Your first step is to limit your topic. No essay — not even a fifty-page paper — can possibly deal effectively with all aspects of any subject, and a writer who does not narrow his topic to workable size defeats himself before he begins.

You will find, if you take the time to think about it, that you have definite ideas about most topics you are assigned. Forcing yourself to formulate your attitudes clearly in your own mind is perhaps the best way to begin limiting a subject.

If, for example, you find that you have definite opinions on a controversial topic, your essay might be designed to convince your readers that you are right. If, on the other hand, you find the subject too complex either to support or to condemn, you might write an essay attempting to clarify it or endeavouring to explain the nature of the complexity to your readers.

Once you have limited your subject, you must decide upon what you intend to accomplish with your essay. No matter what your subject, your handling of it must be designed to lead your readers to the same conclusions you have reached. Unless you are thoroughly familiar with the subject, study will be required to find support for your ideas.

In some cases your teacher will indicate the type and extent of reference work required by the assignment; in other cases these decisions will be left to you. Obviously, however, only you can determine precisely how much factual support will be necessary for your essay to accomplish what you wish. But always keep in mind that, other factors being equal, the student who offers the most relevant facts, apt illustrations, and meaningful examples in support of his assertions will produce the most effective essay.

Do not limit your research of a topic to the most obvious sources of information. Dictionaries and encyclopedias are invaluable, but often newspapers, magazines, and even textbooks or other books will contain more original material and suggest unexplored approaches to your subject.

Suppose, for example, you were asked to write an "at home" essay on "Creativity." After finding a workable definition of the term in a dictionary, you might consult a psychology text or a magazine to find examples of how psychologists encourage creative activities as therapy for the mentally disturbed. An art book would certainly provide examples of artistic creativity, and might also suggest possible new approaches to the subject. Many artists, for example, were also active in other fields: consider the inventor Leonardo da Vinci and the prime minister Winston Churchill. How about an essay proving the value of creative interests by showing how the lives of these men were influenced?

Although some out-of-class essay assignments can be well handled without extensive reading, you will find that only a limited number of concepts and ideas can be validly supported without it. The student from an isolated farm community who has never met a Negro is sadly mistaken if he thinks he can discuss integration without extensive study; without it, his essay could be nothing more than a rehashing of unexamined clichés. The same holds true of any subject you do not know firsthand: No reader will take seriously your analysis of "The Responsibilities of an Executive" unless you show him that your ideas have been formulated after a study of the opinions of experts.

It goes without saying that an at-home essay should be more carefully written and more fully developed than an in-class paper; not even a professional writer can produce the best work of which he is capable without revision and rewriting.

An excellent procedure is to write a first draft of your essay rapidly, paying little attention to mechanics and fine points of style, but being sure that your ideas are arranged in an effective order. Then put the draft aside for as many hours or days as you can spare. When you again pick up the paper, read through it as though it were written by a complete stranger; consider it in terms of what it actually says and how it affects you as an objective reader, rather than in terms of what you know you, as writer, intend. Then begin work on your final copy.

The essays that follow were written by students who were permitted by their instructor to discuss the topic "An International Language." Decide for yourself what each writer attempted to accomplish with his essay and how successful he was in his attempt, before you read the individual commentaries.

1 — AN INTERNATIONAL LANGUAGE

An international language would have its advantages and disadvantages. One of the biggest disadvantages of an international language would be forming it, and the people learning to speak this language besides their native tongue. Probably the greatest advantage of an international language would be in the United Nations because then everyone could understand each other without the interpreters. Since everyone could understand each other, maybe they could solve their problems easier.

Another advantage would be that the people who travel to many countries would not have to know the language of each; they could communicate better through the international language. An international language could discourage the people from learning a foreign language because they know that many people of the world would learn the international language.

When foreign ambassadors come to meet with the prime minister on certain issues, the prime minister and the ambassador could converse without interpreters. The ambassador and prime minister could end the conflict quicker and easier. If the leaders of every country understand each other and solve the problems together, then maybe the chance of war would disappear.

CRITICISM

Discussing a question in terms of its advantages and disadvantages is a basic, and often extremely effective, technique. When an essay is properly organized along these lines, the reader is led to a clear understanding of both sides of the problem, and is able to evaluate for himself the merits of the author's final position on the subject.

This essay is an example of how poor an essay can be if the technique is improperly handled. Instead of leading to comprehension, it confuses any reader who attempts to follow the author's logic.

An "advantage-disadvantage" theme must be organized in one of two ways. The author can divide the body of his paper into two more or less equal parts; the advantages are discussed in one section, the disadvantages in the other. Or, the author may oppose one advantage to a related disadvantage and discuss the pair — and their implications — simultaneously; in this case, pairs follow each other in logical sequence.

No matter which principle is followed, the individual points must be presented in a progressive sequence adapted to the author's purposes in the essay. If, for example, he wishes to conclude that the disadvantages outweigh the advantages, he will be likely to deal with the advantages first and then turn to the disadvantages, for the reader is always most inclined to remember what he has read most recently. Or, the writer may begin his sequence with the most significant disadvantage, followed immediately by a very minor advantage (in order to win the reader to his point of view immediately). In another method of organization, he can devote the central section of his essay to a listing of advantages which, although they are in fact considerably important, would tend to be de-emphasized by the related disadvantages which followed them; his sequence would then end with the second most important disadvantage. Other sequences are, of course, possible; the only rule is that the author follow the logic which most enhances his own point of view.

This essay violates the principles both of organization and logic: the author simply lists his individual points in random order. Although the author's position is clear, the essay makes no attempt to lead the reader to an acceptance of his viewpoint.

The essay is poor in other respects also. The "introduction"— if it is proper to consider the opening sentence as such — makes no attempt to gain the reader's attention or to interest him in the subject: it merely states a truth too obvious to need stating. (Is there *anything* which does not have advantages and disadvantages?)

In addition, the essay abounds in repetition, and its sentence structure and phrasing are awkward. Word choice in the final paragraph is particularly poor: ambassadors come to *meet* with the prime minister *on certain issues* in the first sentence; in sentence two they are trying to *end the conflict;* in the third we are dealing with *the chance of war.* Surely the terms are not synonymous!

EXERCISES

1. The author's presentation of his ideas in the second and third sentences of paragraph one is particularly poor. Grammatical incompleteness is at fault in sentence two; awkward expression obscures the meaning in sentence three. Examine each critically, determine precisely what the author means to say, and then re-write the sentences effectively.

2. Identify and correct all the errors in pronoun agreement throughout the essay.

3. Point out and then eliminate all the repetition of words and phrases.

4. One of the serious weaknesses of the essay is the author's failure to develop any of his points fully. List, in order of importance, both the advantages and disadvantages he mentions and explain how each might have been developed and supported.

5. Write an introduction to the essay which (a) commands the reader's attention; (b) mentions the subject of the theme; (c) implies the author's attitude towards his subject; (d) suggests the organization of the material; and (e) interests the reader in what the author has to say. Delete, if necessary, the author's present opening sentence.

6. Write an appropriate conclusion.

2 — AN INTERNATIONAL LANGUAGE

The first thing to come to my mind when I was asked to write an essay on "An International Language" was "what is the meaning of 'International Language'"? Upon approaching the words "international language" in the dictionary, I found that it meant any natural or artificial language used or designed for international intercourse. For example: Latin was the international language of scholarship until after the close of the Middle Ages, and is still that of the Roman

Catholic Church; French was long that of diplomacy; and English is today virtually that of trade and commerce.

In my opinion, I feel that having an international language would be great. I think that an international language would be wonderful. I think an international language would be great, especially if we ever travel to another country where they do not speak our language. We would not have to worry about knowing someone else's language.

In closing, I say again, if we had an international language, we would be able to speak well with others and would make it easier for people to understand each other.

CRITICISM

This essay, in addition to displaying other weaknesses, exhibits the abuse of another extremely useful organization technique, that of using reference book material as the basis for discussion of a subject.

Quotes or paraphrases, when properly subordinated to the overall purpose of the essay, can be a highly effective means of introducing a topic. A dictionary definition of a word immediately clarifies the sense in which the term is being used and so automatically limits the subject. Encyclopedia materials, on the other hand, concisely define the subject and add authority to any paper.

While it is easy enough to find such quotable materials, it is often difficult to utilize them effectively. No reader is interested in them for their own sake; he cares only about what you do with them, or what you have to say about them. An apt quote or concise paraphrase is mere deadwood if you do not make it serve some function in your essay.

The author of this essay has done absolutely nothing with his search of the dictionary. The material presented in the first paragraph could have been put to any number of uses: he might, for example, have used it to discuss mistaken notions of what an international language is; or he might have used his facts to illustrate the different functions of international languages.

Instead of making his facts work for him, however, he simply dismisses them and ends his essay with a succession of empty phrases.

Another serious fault of the essay is the author's continual use of the first person. The reader has no interest in the first thing that came to the author's mind when he was given an essay assignment; only what he has to say *about* the subject is relevant.

Emphasis on the first person draws attention to the personality of the writer and away from what he has to say. It is a good rule to limit your use of first person to topics on which you are an authority and to essays which deal with your personal reactions to events. For example, a student is obviously an authority on what he observes at school and would be wise — in most cases — to present such observations in the first person. Subjects known only second hand, however, are best discussed in the third person to avoid sounding overly self-centred.

Other weaknesses of the essay are too obvious to merit detailed discussion. The author offers no support for any of his assertions, repeats himself continually, and betrays the fact that he gave no thought to the subject other than that involved in paraphrasing his dictionary.

EXERCISES

1. Locate and correct the error in pronoun agreement in sentence two, paragraph one.

2. The first two sentences are wordy. Rewrite both as concisely as posible.

3. Should the author use quotation marks as he does in the first sentence? Explain. Is the terminal punctuation mark of the same sentence in the correct place? Explain. Why is the colon usage in sentence three incorrect?

4. What is redundant in paragraph two, sentence one?

5. Mark all repetition in the second paragraph.

6. Examine the last sentence in paragraph two. Why is "knowing" an imprecise term?

7. Why should the author not use the phrase "speak well" in the last paragraph?

8. The final sentence is both ungrammatical and awkward. What is the understood subject for the second "would"? What word could be added to make the sentence at least technically correct? How, then, could it be polished into a stylistically smooth and effective concluding sentence?

9. Although the essay says nothing and leads the reader nowhere, it does contain facts, examples, and valid ideas which could be effectively reworked into an essay discussing the function of an international language. Eliminate all the irrelevant first person

references, all the deadwood and repetition. Then, basing your essay on the valuable points which remain, write a unified one-paragraph essay on the function of an international language. If necessary, add a topic sentence, conclusion, or any additional support required to focus your material into an effective presentation of the topic.

10. Do you think that the author in fact found all the material presented in paragraph one in a dictionary? If so, what type of dictionary did he use? If not, where do you think the information was found?

3 — AN INTERNATIONAL LANGUAGE

We all like to think of our time as a period of progression. But are we progressing? Have we removed the barriers to the minds of men? Science has greatly shortened the physical distances by means of advanced modes of transportation, but the distances between the minds of men remain unchanged. Still we are unable to freely exchange our ideas.

We need an international language, a language understood by all. Such a language would allow the removal of the ignorance we all have as to ideas, customs, and feelings of others. Ignorance is the mother of fear. Fear causes war and strife. A means of universally communicating our thoughts and ideas would lower the barriers to the mind, thus abolishing ignorance.

An international language would facilitate the pooling of ideas and further advancement of our society. With so many minds working together, there would be no limit to our achievements.

Perhaps the desire for an international language is far too idealistic. However, more and more people are learning foreign languages and trying to understand the ways of other men. I feel that some type of international language will be employed in the near future.

I believe that when all men of the world can communicate their ideas freely, the intellectual progression of mankind will be astounding.. An international language, more than anything else, might transform the earth into an international brotherhood of peace and prosperity.

CRITICISM

The author of this essay focuses his reader's attention on the abstract rather than on the practical implications of the topic. Such an approach to a subject is often more penetrating and of more universal significance than one which emphasizes everyday considerations, and boggles down in pros and cons, opinions and statistics.

No matter how philosophical or idealistic his outlook, however, a writer must never forget that his readers live in the real world and not in the realm of ideas. Abstractions must be illustrated in concrete, tangible terms to render them meaningful.

The author has neglected to do this. Precisely what does he mean by "barrier to the minds of men"? The phrase could refer to prejudices which prevent rational examination and evaluation of facts. It could, on the other hand, allude to man's inability to express himself fully to others because one's thoughts and perceptions are so intangible. Or, as is probably the case, the phrase might refer to the fact that the same words often mean different things to different people.

The essay is weak in two other respects also. No support is given for many of the author's assertions. If fear, in fact, "causes war and strife," the author should point to at least one case which illustrates this generalization.

In addition, certain points have no perceivable function in the essay, for they do not help lead the reader to the conclusion the author wishes. Paragraph four, for example, is unrelated to the essay as a whole: the points made tell us nothing about the advantages to mankind of an international language, and the author's mention of what "more and more people" are doing seems out of keeping with the otherwise elevated concerns of the essay.

Aside from these weaknesses, the essay is good. It displays a logical mind which presents its thoughts in a sequence designed to lead the reader to a predetermined conclusion.

The prose style is generally mature. The writer employs a variety of sentence constructions, effectively alternates long and short sentences, and (except in paragraph four) permits one sentence to flow smoothly into the next.

EXERCISES

1. Rewrite paragraph one so as to heighten the implied contrast between how progressive we *think* we are and how progressive we *actually* are. (Suggestion: Consider supporting sentence one with a few brief examples before turning your attention to the questions asked in the second and third sentences.) Your revision should make the impact of the final sentence — which introduces the essay topic — more forceful.

2. Paragraph two, which contains the nucleus of the author's argument, is not sufficiently developed with specific examples and details. Rewrite the paragraph adding adequate support for each of the author's assertions.

3. Should the emphasis in the final sentence of paragraph two be on abolishing "ignorance" as the author states, or on abolishing "war"? Defend your answer.

4. Develop paragraph three.

5. Rewrite sentence two of paragraph four, either subordinating the less relevant of the two assertions, or indicating the precise relationship between the two.

6. Examine the word choice in the first sentence of the last paragraph. What does the author mean by "intellectual progression"? Does the term refer to scientific advancements or to something else? How would you clarify his meaning?

4 — AN INTERNATIONAL LANGUAGE

The atomic attack on Hiroshima killed thousands of Japanese and brought intolerable suffering to many others. More tragic than the actual misery it caused, however, is the fact that the bomb was dropped needlessly — the result of a misunderstanding. Why was the bomb dropped?

The United States notified the Japanese that they would drop the atomic bomb unless Japan would agree to peace talks. The official Japanese reply was translated to say that they were going to ignore the U.S. request. Unfortunately, this message was mistranslated: it contained a word which had another English meaning. Actually, the message said that the Japanese needed more time to consider the request. Because of this misunderstanding, thousands of lives were taken that might have been spared. The loss of life alone would have made the effort of constructing a practical international language worthwhile.

More basic than this, an international language can help remove the causes of hatred and wars. It is ignorance and misunderstanding of the customs and feelings of people in other countries which helps to foster hatred. An international language could encourage the free exchange of ideas among people in every part of the world.

That developing and teaching a new language to people throughout the world would be time-consuming is obvious. But I believe the difficulty should not dissuade us, for the price of peace, always high, can be bought only through understanding.

CRITICISM

This is the most effective treatment of the assignment because the author has written his essay for a clearly defined purpose: to convince the reader of the need for an international language. The author's attitude towards the subject is clear and adds force to his prose; implied throughout are the possible consequences to the reader of misunderstanding between nations.

Instead of devoting his introduction to a pedantic statement of his subject and organization, the author immediately gains the reader's attention by a vivid description of one of the major events of the twentieth century. He then discusses this event to show its appropriateness to the subject of the essay. The reader does not discover the actual subject of the essay until after he has been won over to the author's position.

This technique is effective only when the author is able to present a story or an example which is both interesting in itself and an apt illustration of the subject of his essay. While this version of the Hiroshima bombing satisfies both requirements, the reader would be more inclined to accept it as factually true if the author's source were indicated.

The final two paragraphs are less effective than the first part of the essay because they are less specific. Examples should be offered in support of the author's assertions.

Noteworthy is the author's handling of the most obvious major objection to the construction of an international language. Instead of attempting to discount the problems it would entail, he reminds us that anything worthwhile requires effort.

EXERCISES

1. Is the final question in paragraph one necessary? Does it add to or detract from the overall effectiveness of the introduction?

2. Is "request" a good word choice in sentence two, paragraph two? (Consider what is said in the preceding sentence before answering.)

3. To what does the "it" in paragraph two, sentence three, refer? Rewrite and clarify the sentence.

4. Correct the error in agreement in paragraph three.

5. The last two sentences in paragraph three are unsupported and unillustrated assertions. What support might the author have offered for these ideas? Rewrite the paragraph expanding upon and illustrating his points as necessary.

6. Is the author wise or unwise to shift to first person in the final paragraph? Why? Does his use of the phrase "I believe" strengthen or weaken the effect of the essay on the reader?

7. Point out all the ineffective repetition in the essay.

8. The phrasing of the final sentence of the essay is illogical. (A "price" cannot be "bought.") Revise, being careful not to weaken an otherwise effective conclusion.

CHAPTER 2

THE "IN CLASS" ESSAY ASSIGNMENT

One can accomplish only so much during a class period. Your teacher is well aware of the time limitations imposed upon you when he asks you to write an impromptu essay, and he expects no more of you than is reasonable.

The key to writing a successful impromptu is — as should be fairly obvious — the wisest and most efficient use of the time available. The ways of putting this rule into practice, however, may not be quite as obvious, and some suggestions may prove useful.

Since every essay you write must accomplish something — make its point in the most effective manner possible — you must follow the same steps no matter how much time you have at your disposal. When faced with writing an impromptu, you must decide rapidly what you wish your essay to accomplish, outline (either mentally or on paper) the means you will use to achieve your purpose, find support for the assertions you will make, organize your material coherently, and write in a style and tone appropriate to your subject. Quite a few chores, yes. But no more than you can handle if you utilize your time efficiently.

The major problem in writing an impromptu is finding adequate support for your ideas. For, except when you have been forewarned of the topic, no advance study is possible. It is, nevertheless mandatory that you offer to your readers the facts, illustrations, and examples necessary to substantiate your ideas.

Since you cannot resort to books for information, support must be found in your own background and experiences. If you pause for a moment before beginning your essay with the first words which come into your head, you will certainly discover that the resources at your disposal are more than adequate.

Consider, for example, just a few of the uses to which you might put a discussion of the way your mother prepares or serves dinner. If her cooking differs in the slightest way from everyone else's, you could present this difference as an example of individuality, as an illustration of creativity, or as a fact in support of the assertion that there is no such thing as a "typical housewife". If, on the other hand, you chose to emphasize how similar to everyone else's cooking your mother's is, you would have fine support for an essay arguing that individuality no longer exists, or that the goal of many people is to be as like their neighbours in as many ways as possible. The reasons she buys certain foods at certain stores could be offered in a theme on economics; the manner in which she serves dinner might indicate something of the structure of the typical (or atypical) family; grace — or the absence of it — before meals could illustrate the actual function of religion in our daily lives. Obviously, the possibilities are limitless.

Making the most efficient use of the time available for an impromptu is, as mentioned earlier, essential. Many successful writers find the following techniques useful.

After deciding how you will approach the assignment and outlining the development of your essay, keep in mind that you may not, after all, have time to finish. Therefore do not state specifically what you will do in your introduction. Instead, write an introduction which, while interesting your readers in the topic, permits you to expand upon or abbreviate your material as time permits. In other words, avoid saying specifically that you will do thus and so in the essay; rather, tell your readers what you will talk about.

The conclusion to an essay is always the most important section. It is here, if anywhere, that you finally convince the reader that your ideas are valid; in addition, every word in the essay should lead almost inevitably to your conclusion. Because of this, it is often wise to sketch in your conclusion *before* writing the body of the essay.

This practice is useful for a number of reasons. In the first place, if you know precisely where the essay is leading, you will be more inclined to focus the body of your paper effectively. Secondly, should your time run short, you will not find yourself searching desperately for an effective ending.

Finally, the most satisfactory organization for an impromptu is often one which follows the pattern of a news story. Following your introduction, make your points without going into detail about them. Then elaborate on them and offer support for them in a logical sequence. In this way, even if you cannot finish your essay, your major ideas will have been stated, and the most important issues discussed in detail. If anything must be sacrificed in impromptu writing, it should be discussion of your least essential material.

The essays which follow were all written during a single class period. Students had no idea of the essay topic before entering class.

1 — THE BEST THINGS IN LIFE ARE FREE
Imagine anyone going into a store and after purchasing some products, they receive S & H Green Stamps, Golden Bell Stamps, High-Low Stamps, Orange Stamps, Protection Stamps, stamps for receiving a certain number of stamps, or any type of stamp the store happens to be giving away that month. If a person collects one thousand stamps and puts them into a free stamp book, he can redeem them for a ping-pong ball; with 15,000 stamps someone can get a stuffed teddy bear; and with 1,254,991,783 stamps anyone can get a personally autographed picture of Charles de Gaulle. All of these amazing items can be obtained with stamps that are given away.

To get the best things in life faster than by saving stamps, all someone needs to do is steal whatever they desire. This is a very simple and easy way because a person doesn't have to have brains in order to steal. If someone steals valuable objects, he can buy a car, mink coat, a girl friend, nice clothes, 1,254,991,783 stamps, and an education — in the house of correction.

One does not have to pay for oil, pearls, natural gas, diamonds, and petroleum if they happen to be on one's land. Police protection, fire protection, zoos, parks, and Labor Day parades are free. Anyone can go to the beach and take home as much sand as they desire and it will not cost them a penny. You can date a girl and spend thousands of dollars on her but the love she gives you is free, as long as you continue to take her out. Our glorious country paid for its right to liberty so that everyone could be free to pay taxes. The best things in life are free?

CRITICISM
The author of this theme has tried desperately — *too* desperately, perhaps — to make his point through humor, and has succeeded only in revealing how confused his thinking is. One "gag" after another

does not necessarily add up to a comic paper, just as an endless succession of pies thrown in a clown's face does not strike the viewer as funny. A lemon pie or two may make us laugh; too many pies may appear sadistic.

The essay as a whole is a failure because the author fails to accomplish anything with it. He does not clarify the object of his satire: Is he poking fun at the person who saves trading stamps, or at the concept that "the best things in life are free"?

The opening words of the essay — "Imagine anyone going into a store" — suggest what might have been an effective means of achieving humour. Had the author permitted us to visualize a Mrs. Befuddled buying things she doesn't need simply to obtain trading stamps, and then gleefully exchanging them for some object which we (the readers) recognize as worthless, both the person who is deluded by the idea he can get something for nothing, as well as the idea itself, might have been pointedly ridiculed.

As it is, the author tries to force us to laugh by piling exaggeration upon exaggeration. The truth, slightly overstated, can be funny; one absurdity following another turns initial amusement into contempt.

Ironically, the author, in his attempts to force laughter, overlooks the inherent humour in the situation he presents. No matter how the situations were presented, exposure of the consumer's tendency to buy unwisely simply to obtain a nice gift which is clearly worth much less than the money wasted on unnecessary or overpriced merchandise would be funny.

In addition to these fundamental flaws, the author follows no chain of logic. In spite of the fact that he attempts to cover up his lack of coherence by the transition between paragraphs one and two, a reader immediately sees that there is no connection between trading stamps and stealing. He also ignores the rather obvious fact that it does take brains to get the best things in life by stealing — and not get caught.

EXERCISES

1. The essay is filled with shifts in person, with errors in agreement and with awkward passive construction. Find and correct all such grammatical errors. Be prepared to defend the effectiveness, as well as the correctness, of your revisions.

2. As a summary of what the author has described in paragraph one, the phrase "all of these amazing items" in the final sentence is extremely poor. Why? Find a substitute.

3. Paragraph one is an unsuccessful attempt at humour through exaggeration. Following the suggestions in the Criticism, rewrite the paragraph so as to make it both funny as well as functional in the theme.

4. Assuming that the author's purpose in this theme is to show that the best things in life are *not* free by implying ironically that people only think they are getting something for nothing, rewrite every sentence in the essay which does not help him achieve his aim.

5. After completing exercise four, refocus each paragraph to make it subordinate to the author's overall purpose.

2 — ARE THE BEST THINGS IN LIFE FREE?

I am a dreamer who loves to think while lying on a quiet hill. I am an adventurer who loves stalking a wild animal in the woods, matching wits with Nature herself to see which team, the man and his gun, or the deer and his instincts, will win. Reclining in a boat on a quiet lake, walking through the woods, or watching the sun come up: these things I cherish most. To me they are the best things that life has to offer, and they do not cost a cent. However, when I bring a companion along to enjoy that same sunrise, he is unimpressed. I realize then that not all people value these things in the same way. My friend's taste is quite different from mine.

My pal is a dreamer too, but he loves to lie in bed thinking of all the great fun he will have on his next date. He is an adventurer also, but he enjoys whizzing around corners in a big, fat car. Sitting on the deck of a yacht sipping cocktails, telling "warmed-over" jokes at a "swinging" party, shooting pool every other night: to him these are the best things in life. Everything that he values has a price on it.

Even though there is no price tag on watching the sunrise or walking in the woods, are these things really free? "Free" as Webster defines it means not only "without cost or payment," but also "not under the control of some person or some arbitrary power." Herein lies the answer. The things in life that I love most are without cost; I am not under the control of some other person; but I am under the control of some arbitrary power. This power is myself.

Some can freely take off and chase their fancy by living the romantic life of the woodsman, but I cannot. The quality that must be examined here is security. I must be secure in my occupation, home, and community. I must have the assurance that I can enjoy these pleasures of life and yet know that I am not evading reality. For me the "free" that is restricting in this statement is not the free from "free ticket" but the free from "free mind". Therefore I do not and I cannot believe that the best things in life are free.

CRITICISM

This essay, in spite of some excellent writing and the author's effective handling of certain difficult techniques, is not altogether successful. Its relative failure can be traced to the author's shifting his line of development halfway through the essay.

The essay attempts to achieve its effect by means of contrasts, and insofar as the author follows this technique, the essay is successful. Note that the values presented in the second paragraph are carefully opposed to those in paragraph one; each description of the "pal" is introduced by a word used earlier. The overall effect is a balanced and emphatic contrast between the two friends.

These two paragraphs of course lead the reader to expect a discussion of the opposed values and interests and, possibly, even a reconciliation of the two. The reader is thus totally confused when the author leads him off in an entirely different direction in paragraph three.

Instead of using the dictionary definition of "free" to elucidate the material presented earlier, the author completely dismisses his "pal" and focuses attention on the fact that he, himself, is not free. From this point on, the term "free" is not used to evaluate, but rather to define the author.

But does the author's discussion of himself and his inability to grasp the "free" things he wants because he is not "free" interest us? More importantly, does it shed light on the essay topic?

Clearly not, for the author, in his concern with proving that he is not free, overlooks what is fairly obvious to anyone who has ever taken a vacation. Most people are able to have both security and freedom. One does not "evade reality" by occasionally "lying on a quiet hill" or "matching wits with Nature".

Thus the author of this essay, because he did not discuss the materials he presented early in the essay, and because he permitted himself to get carried away by a play on words, destroyed the overall effectiveness of an essay which began very well.

Certain specific elements in the essay deserve praise. Writing in the first person is seldom successful, for most authors do not subordinate their own personalities to the purpose of the essay. Here the technique is effectively handled. The author presents only aspects of himself (or his fictional "self") which have a definite function in the essay. As noted earlier, however, the "I" of the first paragraph has an entirely different function from the later "I".

In addition, the author's word choice and phrasing in the first two paragraphs are excellent. Vivid terms permit the reader to see precisely what is being described. There is a fine variety of sentence structure, and a smooth flow to the prose.

EXERCISES

1. Point out and distinguish between all the effective and all the ineffective repetition in the theme. Be prepared to defend your choices.

2. Discuss the sentence variety in the first two paragraphs. Is variety achieved in any cases at the expense of proper emphasis?

3. In paragraph two, does the fact that the friend's jokes are termed "warmed over" contribute to or detract from the picture we get of him?

4. Does the author's use of the term "warmed over" contribute to or detract from the contrast he wishes to emphasize between his friend and himself?

5. Would the contrast between the two be more effective in the overall theme if both were described completely objectively? Point out the words in each paragraph which betray subjective evaluations of the activities of each.

6. Should either or both the terms "warmed over" and "swinging" be in quotes? Why or why not?

7. Rewrite and refocus paragraphs three and four so that the essay effectively makes the point which the author intends. (See Criticism for an explanation of what this is.)

8. Do you think either or both the "I" character and the friend exist in real life? Is either or both a creation of the author? Defend your opinions.

3 — ARE THE BEST THINGS IN LIFE FREE?

Probably the oldest trick in selling is the free gift gimmick. For simply letting the salesman in and listening to his sales pitch you will receive a small, practical, usually inexpensive gift. The salesman said the gift was free when you opened the door, but after you have wasted valuable time listening to his boring talk, or have bought a product which you didn't really need, you wonder whether that little gift was really free or not. So it is with most seemingly free things in life. "Are the best things in life free?" can only be answered within oneself.

First we must define our terms. What are "the best things"? Is success the best thing? Is living a life of leisure — one without responsibilities, worries, problems — the best thing in life? To define "the best things" with simplification, let us say that they are the most desirable. To many, love is the best thing in life. To obtain love — and I use "obtain" meaningfully — could be the best thing in life, for true unselfish love is indeed a treasure. But how many people who have been loved and had it free, that is, didn't give of themselves to receive it, how many of these people treasure that love?

Then there is the word "free." Free can mean without cost, but without cost of what? Money? Time? Patience? Is anything really free? Let's look at scenery; scenery is supposed to be free, but we first have to get to where the scenery is located before we can look. Then, we may have to climb a hillside before we can look at "free" scenery. If we are sticklers for meaning we can say the scenery is not free because being able to appreciate it involves effort — travelling, climbing, and looking.

Now back to the original but revised question. Are the most desirable things in life without cost? I say no. Anything that is worth having will not be free. Something that is free loses its charm, its colour, its flare, and its desirability. Most things that are desirable are the product of many years of work, much hardship, much pain, and much effort. The best things are most desirable because of these hardships.

CRITICISM

This is the most effective handling of the essay topic because it is the most mature in concept. Instead of either attacking or defending the obvious cliché, the author examines its implications.

The introduction is excellent. To gain his reader's interest, the author begins with an evaluation of a situation which is familiar to all, and which aptly illustrates the thesis developed by the essay as a whole. The discussion that follows is an examination of the lesson exemplified by the anecdote.

Analysis of the structure of the remainder of the essay suggests that the author lost control of his material while writing. He admits that the terms in question must be defined, and then offers what he admits to be oversimplified definitions of them. His final paragraph which offers a valid appraisal of the entire quote, is designed to emphasize the inadequacy of the commonly accepted notions discussed in the two central paragraphs.

Paragraph two, unfortunately, does not fulfill its function in this development. The example chosen to shed light on "the best things" instead focuses attention on the meaning of the term "free."

To fully carry out the task he had set for himself, the author should have handled paragraph two in much the same way as he did paragraph three. In other words, he should show here that what are commonly accepted as "the best things" are not, in fact, worth having at all.

EXERCISES
1. The last sentence in paragraph one appears to have little relationship either to the rest of the paragraph or to what follows in paragraph two. Does the sentence serve a function in the essay? If so, defend its inclusion. Comment also on its placement.
2. Rewrite paragraph two in light of the Criticism.
3. Rewrite the last paragraph, eliminating any weaknesses in diction, and more effectively emphasizing the point the author wishes to make.

CHAPTER 3
THE ESSAY OF DEFINITION
Since words are arbitrary symbols, they are valuable to communication only when they mean precisely the same thing to both user and audience. Problems in communication seldom arise when we use terms which symbolize objects which have concrete reality: *cow, gold, ocean*. Problems do arise, however, when we must express ourselves about intangibles, for often words which mean one thing to us mean something entirely different to others.

Take, for example, the abstract term "freedom." Were you to write an essay arguing that freedom is good (a sentiment we all take for granted) without first clearly defining what you meant by "freedom," just consider some of the ways different readers might interpret your ideas.

A thief might believe you to be saying that he is *free* to steal anything he likes, and that no one (especially the police) has a right to interfere with this *freedom*. A philosopher might think you were talking about the *freedom* of the mind; an editor, about *freedom* of the press; a theologian, about *freedom* of religion. Coming closer to home, your father might think you were suggesting that he *free* himself from his responsibilities to his family and, instead of going to work every day, devote himself solely to his hobbies. Your mother (who perhaps considers housekeeping an unpleasant but necessary chore) might agree that in the future you should be *free* to cook your own meals and clean up your own messes. Obviously, then, if you permitted your readers to interpret "freedom" any way they chose, you would accomplish precisely the reverse of what you attempted in your essay.

Anarchy of this sort can be avoided only by making clear to your readers precisely what the abstract terms you use are intended to symbolize. In other words, you must define such abstractions in terms meaningful to your readers.

Definitions, however, must always be subordinated to the overall purposes of your essays. A long and very precise definition of "freedom" in the abstract would have no place in an essay designed to show your readers that students should be permitted to express in school newspapers opinions contrary to those of their teachers. In such an essay, a few words indicating that you were concerned only with the freedom to disagree with the opinions of others in certain circumstances are all that would be required. Your definition would consist merely of limiting the meaning of the term.

In other cases, devoting an entire essay to defining and illustrating a key term may be the most effective means of dealing with a topic. Such essays are often designed to (1) explain esoteric terms which you feel should be in your readers' vocabularies; (2) discuss a word which people use daily without really comprehending its meaning, implications, or connotations; (3) contrast the actual meaning (its "denotation") of a word to its connotations; or (4) illustrate some misconceptions about the meaning of a word. Other functions, however, are also possible.

The methods which will best accomplish your purpose depend upon your subject, for any technique which will assist you in clarifying a word or concept may be used in a definition essay. One rule — and only one — need be followed: every word used, every example offered, must be designed to lead your reader to a clearer understanding of the topic under consideration.

Note that essays 2 and 3 of Chapter 2, and the first essay in this chapter, all subordinate definitions to other aspects of their topics. Essays 2 and 3, on the other hand, attempt to communicate solely by means of definition.

1 — JUSTICE

In the past, two men were charged with murdering their wives. Each was tried in court and convicted — one was sentenced to five years in prison, and the other was sentenced to death in the electric chair. Each man gave proof that his wife was unfaithful, yet refused to give him a divorce. Arriving home unexpectedly, each man found his wife in the company of her lover; both husbands flew into a rage and stabbed and killed their wives.

These two instances happened under practically identical circumstances to college educated men who had no previous criminal record. The punishment for these men was not similar at all. In at least one case, or possibly in both, the punishment was unjust.

Reasons to allow for the indifference in the punishment of the two criminals could be the different ways the lawyers and prosecutors presented their cases. Feelings of the juries towards the murders must be taken into consideration. Some jurymen would have sympathy toward the dead wives, while the others would have it for the husbands. Whether or not the judge was for or against the death penalty is another factor.

In the trial of the first man, the judge presiding had never given a death sentence for it was against his beliefs. The jury was composed of two males and a female who had gotten divorces and knew how it felt to be unhappy with one's mate. The lawyer in this case had a fine winning record for his clients and knew to appeal to the jury for sympathy and pity. The man was sentenced to a mere five years in prison. The time the other case appeared in court there was a different conglomeration of jurymen, lawyers, and a judge. The judge was well known for quickly giving the death sentence. The district attorney was a capable and experienced man while the defense attorney was fresh out of college. The jury — composed of happily married men and women — rapidly agreed this offense was a great sin.

Webster talks about justice as maintenance or administration that is just in accordance to rules of equality or the principle of rectitude and just dealing. To reach this level of justice a court must be completely stripped of all appeals to sympathy and pity. The court must stick to the laws pertaining to the trial proceedings and punishment. In the analogy of unjustice the courts failed to do this and look what happened.

CRITICISM

Although the material presented by the author is interesting and generally well-handled, Essay 1 must, in the final analysis, be considered a failure. It does not accomplish the purpose for which it was written.

The author *intended* to lead his readers to a clearer understanding of "justice". The raw materials selected to achieve this purpose are excellent: the two trials clearly illustrate the fact that our judge and jury system does not always provide "justice"; the dictionary definition at the end is a fine basis for a discussion of the topic. In addition, the author's conclusions are valid: based on the evidence presented, both men certainly did not receive equal justice.

What went wrong?

The author, while writing his essay, lost sight of his overall intentions, and permitted himself to become overly interested in material which is, after all, only an example. The focus of the essay is on the illustration, rather than on the principle which the illustration was designed to reveal. The author shows why the two trials came out as they did, but he tells us nothing about "justice."

The essay could be successfully rewritten in a number of ways. An introduction announcing the subject under discussion, followed by an indication that the analysis of the two trials was an example of the way in which justice may be abused, would permit the reader to see the elements of the essay in proper perspective.

If, on the other hand, the author preferred to begin with the example, he could refocus his essay by beginning paragraph two with a statement stressing the function of the example in the essay; the final paragraph, then, should discuss the relevance of the example to the concept "justice" in general.

In any case, the essay as it stands is an example of the kind of trouble you are likely to get into if you do not properly subordinate the individual elements of your essay to your purposes for writing.

EXERCISES

1. After considering our criticism of this essay, rewrite it so that it accomplishes the purpose for which it was intended. Incorporate whichever of the following exercises seem necessary into your revision.

2. Is the sequence of "facts" in the first two paragraphs logical? Is it effective? Consider possible rearrangements of the individual

sentences (reworded, or course, as necessary), and discuss the relative advantages and disadvantages of different sequences.

3. What is the function of paragraph three in the overall structure of the essay? Does it accomplish its purpose?

4. It is not clear until the middle of paragraph four just which of the two is "the first man". How could the author have clarified this point?

5. Certain words in the essay do not convey the meanings intended by the author. Two examples are "indifference" in the first sentence of paragraph three, and "injustice" in the last sentence of the essay. What, precisely, does the author mean by these terms? Correct these and any other poor word choices you find.

6. A dictionary definition often requires clarification, discussion, and illustration by the author of an essay. If you think such is the case in this essay, elaborate on the definition in the final paragraph as necessary.

7. Does the author mean, as he implies, that the jury mentioned at the beginning of paragraph four consisted of *only* "two males and a female"? Revise and clarify. Consider also his usage of the terms "male" and "female" in this context. Do they add to or detract from what he is saying?

2 — LOVE

He drew a circle that shut me out
Heretic, rebel, a thing to flout.
But Love and I had the wit to win:
We drew a circle that took him in!

This poem entitled "Outwitted" by Edwin Markham implies that love is a brotherly affection. The dictionary says that love is a feeling of fondness or attachment for another person. Actually love is not one but many things. It can mean charity, friendship, devotion, or loyalty. Love has been called the most important word in any language; however, it is also the most misunderstood word of all. People often say that they love a good book or that they love a particular piece of clothing. When used in this sense, not love but desire or enjoyment is expressed. While this does imply like or dislike, it does not connote the true meaning of the word.

Perhaps the Greeks had the best way of all for expressing the varying degrees of our word "love." "Eros" meant love of self. This is that which manifests itself in what we term self-centeredness. In this type of love a person is concerned only with himself. Although he knows a form of love, he does not receive love to a great extent. This is perhaps sadder than not knowing how to love. "Philia" is another Greek word for love used to define the brotherly type of love. This is what is now known as feeling toward another person as one would feel toward a brother or close relative. The last word used in the Greek language to express love is the word "agape" which means selfless love. I think that this is the type of love which Christ meant when He said, "Greater love hath no man than this, that a man lay down his life for his friends".

This last type of love is the most important of all and involves varying aspects. When used with this meaning, love is giving. In this form love is ironic, for only by the giving of oneself in love can one ever hope to gain inner peace. The giving of one's knowledge, skill, sympathy, or friendship is an act of true love. Caring enough to give is an essential ingredient for selfless love. To care enough to give of one's time or effort is a result of love. The Italian expression for love denotes this same meaning. "Ti voglio bene" means "I desire your well-being." To be a loving person one must love enough to put another's well being above one's own. Love is the act of giving oneself up to the desire of happiness for others. It is putting their happiness above one's own.

It seems to me that love is that which separates man from those things which are less than human. A computer can now think, and an animal can perform the duties necessary for self-preservation and well-being. However, man is the only animal which is capable of love or concern for other beings. Without love, man is nothing more than a sub-human animal fulfilling animal-like desires. This is verified in the *Bible* in First Corinthians: "And though I have the gift of prophecy and understand all mysteries, and all knowledge; and though I have all faith, so that I could remove mountains, and have not love, I am nothing".

Personally, I feel that love is that which "Beareth all things, believeth all things, hopeth all things, endureth all things".

CRITICISM

This essay illustrates the "scholarly approach" to the definition essay assignment. We will be better able to appreciate the strengths and weaknesses of the composition if we consider certain aspects of the method in general before turning our attention to the essay itself.

Research and evaluation must, of course, precede the writing of such essays. The author begins work by searching for as many different definitions of the term, as well as illustrations of its various usages, as possible. He is under no obligation to incorporate every bit of information he finds into his final essay, but, if he wishes to do a good job, he will utilize as much — and no more — of this material as will lead his readers to a clear comprehension of the total meaning of the concept under discussion.

When selecting the definitions and illustrations to be included in the essay, the writer must carefully analyze the relationships between them. Very often one definition will tend to contradict another; one usage may clarify an overly abstruse definition; another illustration may modify and qualify an oversimplified definition. The author must explicitly or implicitly indicate the light each sheds on the others, and show the relative significance of each to the comprehensive definition with which his essay is concerned.

The diverse materials used in such essays may be organized in any number of ways, so long as some consistent principle is followed. One technique is to present the definitions and usages in chronological order, thus leading the reader to an understanding of how the current meaning has evolved. Another possibility is development by contrasts: the writer concentrates on examining the paradoxes and contradictions implied by various parts of his raw materials. Such essays often lead the reader to an appreciation of the complexity of the term under discussion.

Yet another way is to lead the reader from a consideration of the diverse meanings of the term to a comprehension of its essence. In this case, the writer separates the implications of various usages from the central meanings.

Whichever line of development is followed, however, the author must see to it that every piece of material he offers has a definite function in his essay. Each definition or illustration must be related to the others used, and each must add something to the reader's overall understanding of the term. None may be treated in isolation, for isolated instances tend to confuse rather than inform.

The author of Essay 2 has presented some excellent material, but he has not paid sufficient attention either to relationships between individual definitions or to overall organization. The essay argues that the "agape" form of love is most important, but does not show the bearing of all the other definitions and usages upon this argument.

Beginning an essay of this style with a quote is a fine technique, but the quote must be made to function in the essay as a whole. It is not clear whether or not we are to see the dictionary definition (paragraph one, sentence two) as a contrast to the definition implied by the quote, or as an elaboration of it.

The entire first paragraph is confusing because the author's topic sentence — the third — neither introduces the diverse meanings of "love" offered nor summarizes them. Had the author stressed the central idea of the paragraph, the relationships between sentences would be clear, and the paragraph would have served a definite function in the essay.

The material presented in paragraph two is excellent, but the introduction to the material is poor. The important point is that the Greeks had three separate terms for "love", and that each of these defines a type of love within our own experience. In the paragraph, though, the reader is left wondering which — if any — of the Greek terms could be applied to the various meanings of "love" offered in paragraph one. Is the love of a good book either "eros", "philia", or "agape"? If none of these, do we use the term incorrectly in such a sense?

The conclusion of the essay is perhaps its weakest single element. The author offers the *Bible* as proof for his argument, but does not consider those of his readers who do not believe in the literal truth of the *Bible*. An objective reader would accept Biblical verification only if the author showed why, and in what sense, the *Bible* is an authority on the subject.

In addition, the final sentence of the essay makes the entire essay subjective. A reader is concerned with why he should agree with the author, not with what the author "personally" feels about a subject.

EXERCISES

As pointed out in the Criticism section, paragraph one is unfocused and should be rewritten. Consider the following possibilities, and compare and contrast their effectiveness.

Revision A: Beginning with a quote —

1. The author does not support his assertion that the poem "implies that love is a brotherly affection." If you agree that it does, add a sentence or two supporting this interpretation. If you disagree, what aspect of love *does* the poem illustrate?

2. Indicate the relationships between each sentence, rewriting and shifting their order as necessary.

Revision B: Beginning with a topic sentence —

3. Rewrite the entire paragraph beginning with the sentence, "Love has been called the most important word in any language; however, it is also the most misunderstood word of all". Shift the material presented — adding and deleting as necessary — so that the entire paragraph proves the truth of this paradox.

4. Rewrite the entire paragraph beginning with the sentence, "Love is not one but many things". Rewrite individual sentences so that all the material presented supports this assertion. Add illustrations as necessary.

Paragraph two —

5. Break this paragraph into three separate new paragraphs, illustrating each Greek term with one or more contemporary examples. Draw on, or refer back to, material presented in paragraph one as necessary.

6. Clarify the meaning of sentence five.

7. Explain and illustrate the meaning of sentence six.

8. Show why the "eros" type of love is "sadder than not knowing how to love".

9. Is the "agape" type of love in any way different from what the author says elsewhere of "brotherly love"? Clarify the precise relationship between the two types, or show that they are identical.

Paragraph three —

10. Support the author's assertion that the "agape" type of love is "the most important".

11. Explain what the author means by "ironic" in sentence three.

12. Is the repetition in sentences five and six effective? Why or why not?

13. Introduce the Biblical quotation in paragraph four showing its correct relationship to the subject of the theme. (If it does not "verify" the author's assertions, precisely what *does* it do?)

14. Write a conclusion which shows the significance to the reader of all the author has said in the essay.

3 — HONESTY

Honesty is a word which comes up everyday in discussing current affairs. Under question is honesty in top places, honesty in

40

local officials and honesty of businessmen and merchants. Everyone is always watching these important men so that they have no chance to go astray. But what about the people themselves? Are they as honest as they could be? Many who claim to be honest, upright citizens are actually petty thieves stealing from the government in the form of false income tax returns, keeping money gained by the mistakes of others and evading everything they possibly can.

True honesty is not hard to discern in any individual for it pops out in the little things he does. If he is undercharged by the grocer he wouldn't think of keeping this small profit. When filling out his tax returns he lists every income no matter how obscure. He actually goes out of his way to be as honest as possible rather than taking advantage of any possible gain. Honesty is *not* just doing what one is told when everyone is keeping an eye on him, for in this situation one can do nothing except what is right. However, if a person who is not being carefully watched has a chance to get ahead through dishonesty but still does the right thing, he is practicing real honesty. Honesty is *not* simply conforming to certain standards set by the general public. This could be classed under the quality of being law-abiding rather than being honest. Honesty must be an inner quality, not just a show put on by someone who wishes to impress others.

In other words, to be *really* honest one needs always to keep in mind the difference between right and wrong. Honesty must be a guiding policy all through life. In every little incident of life the problem of honesty comes up.

CRITICISM

Although weak in diction, this essay is the most effective of the three because the author subordinates everything he says to his purpose in writing.

The first paragraph is good because it effectively limits the topic. The author tells us that he will be discussing and defining "honesty" in specific contexts; everything will be related to "the people themselves" rather than to "important men" who have little opportunity for dishonesty in the first place.

The first sentence of paragraph two states a principle which is illustrated and discussed throughout. In addition, note that each illustration permits the author to make a fine distinction between "true honesty" and the type of honesty which is not "an inner quality". These distinctions lead inevitably to the conclusion that honesty is a quality of mind rather than a pattern of behaviour.

EXERCISES

The overall development of this essay is excellent, but many individual sentences are awkward and detract from the essay's effectiveness. The following exercises deal with these weaknesses in diction.

1. Sentences one and two: Rewrite, making the opening lines more dynamic and direct. Review the rhetorical functions of an Introduction before making your revisions.

2. Sentence three: Where is/are the antecedent(s) for "these important men"? What, precisely, is wrong with this sentence? Correct it.

3. Sentence four: Is it clear to *which* specific people the author refers? Rewrite and clarify if necessary.

4. Sentence six: Rewrite the sentence so it reads, ". . . thieves who steal . . . who keep money . . . who evade . . ." Is such a sentence structure more or less effective? Why? Can you think of other effective ways to recast the sentence?

Paragraph two:

5. Sentence one: Why is the phrase "pops out" stylistically inappropriate in this theme? Find a better phrase.

6. Sentence one: Rewrite the sentence presenting the author's idea in two independent clauses, the second of which explains the first. Which of the three mechanically correct punctuation marks (";" ":" or "—") would be most effective? Why?

7. Sentence four: This sentence is ungrammatical. How? Rewrite.

8. Sentences five through nine: Where is the author's phrasing particularly poor? Rewrite the entire section, making everything which *is* honest structurally parallel to all which *is not* honest. How does this parallelism add to the effectiveness of the essay?

9. The entire conclusion — and especially the last sentence — is very weak. Write a more dynamic final paragraph.

CHAPTER 4

THE CHARACTER SKETCH

There are only two distinctively different types of character sketch, but innumerable subspecies of each type. They come in all sizes and all shapes, and can serve any one of a number of functions in student writing. Space will permit no more than a rapid survey of the more common varieties, and some hints about the uses to which they may be put.

One variety of character sketch differentiates the individual person from all others; its function is to communicate to the reader the "essence" of a character's individuality. The other variety does the converse: it highlights the characteristics shared by all individuals of a certain class. An author's purpose in writing, of course, determines which type will best suit his needs in a particular assignment.

Any person — real or fictitious — about whom you have some knowledge can serve as the subject of the sketch of an individual. A friend, a relative, a character from a book, even yourself; any may be suitable.

The important thing to remember is that while your character will not differ in all respects from everyone else — we are, after all, human, and each of us has pretty much the same organs, senses, fears and desires — the essence of your subject's personality is strictly his own, and it is this to which you must draw attention.

For example, nearly every student's grandfather is about the age of the subject of Essay 2, but only that particular grandfather enjoys hunting in spite of the fact that he is partially deaf, and only he has developed the traits of honesty, sincerity, and straightforwardness as the results of an unhappy childhood combined with an unfortunate disability in youth. The essay draws attention to the unique aspects of the man, but suggests that he is like other men in other respects.

Essay 3, on the other hand, deals with types of people rather than with individuals. The author attempts to accomplish his purpose (showing that there is a correlation between the way high school students dress and their intellectual motivations) by emphasizing the characteristics which most members of the groups he mentions have in common.

While no single individual would behave in all respects as does the "typical" member of his class, each does have more in common with his group than with any other. Thus, if the author's observations are accurate and his presentation effective, the reader should be able to place any individual high school student he meets into one of the categories set up in the essay.

Either type of character sketch may be as long or as short as suits a writer's purposes. The first two in this section are essay length since their authors were concerned solely with character analysis; essay 3, on the other hand, incorporates three separate, but related, sketches because the author was interested not in character itself, but rather in the differences between types of characters.

The chief prerequisite to writing a character sketch is to be perfectly clear about your reasons for writing about the individual or type of person you choose, for different aspects of character are, of course, emphasized for different purposes. Once you know what you wish your sketch to accomplish, all you must do is be certain that the picture you present is clear enough for the reader to visualize, but not cluttered with details which detract from the overall purpose.

1 — ARTHUR DIMMESDALE

To my mind, the most noteworthy character of *The Scarlet Letter* is Arthur Dimmesdale. In fact, it seems that the purpose of the novel is to examine the minister's torment and contrast it with the fate of his partner in sin, Hester Prynne.

He is an unusual character because, in spite of his obsession with good and bad, he is unable to confess his crime of adultery. There is an indication, however, that Dimmesdale believed that a confession would be wrong, and is tormented only by the initial act. In Chapter ten, while Dimmesdale and Chillingworth are discussing why some men will hide their sins all their life, Dimmesdale comments, "Guilty as they may be, retaining, nevertheless, a zeal for God's glory and man's welfare, they shrink from displaying themselves black and filthy in the view of men; because, thenceforward, no good can be achieved by them; no evil of the past be redeemed by better service".

But whether Dimmesdale urgently wants to confess or not, his appearance betrays great inner strife. He is pale and drawn and so nervous that Hester wonders if he is still sane.

CRITICISM

This essay is unsuccessful because, while the author has some interesting points to make about the character of Dimmesdale, these are not supported, and the essay as a whole is unfocused.

Any introduction should always give the reader some indication of the subject of the essay which follows. This introduction, however, presents two unrelated points, neither of which is in any way developed or illustrated in the essay. We are never shown why the writer considers Dimmesdale "noteworthy", nor are we given any support for the author's thesis about the purpose of the novel as a whole.

The second paragraph, although unrelated to the essay itself, has some merit. Here the author illustrates by an apt quote Dimmesdale's attitude towards confession. The quote itself is well introduced by a discussion of its function in the paragraph, and by an indication of where it occurs in the novel.

The major weakness in the paragraph is the opening phrase. The material presented in no way shows why Dimmesdale is "unusual".

The final paragraph is as poor as the first, for the author does not say enough about his character's "appearance" to make his point. Had we been told that Dimmesdale was previously the converse of the way he is now described, we might accept the writer's assertion that his appearance *now* betrays "inner strife". As presented, however, the details of his appearance prove nothing, for some people are "pale, drawn, and nervous" all their lives.

Note that even if each of the unsupported assertions in the essay were sufficiently developed, the organization would still detract from the essay's effectiveness. A logically presented character sketch of this type might describe the physical appearance of its subject, then discuss the implications of his appearance, and finally show the function of these details in the novel as a whole.

EXERCISES

The following exercises are designed for students who are familiar with *The Scarlet Letter*.

1. List in outline form support for the author's assertion that "the purpose of the novel is to examine the minister's torment and contrast it with the fate of . . . Hester Prynne".

2. Decide upon the most effective sequence for the presentation and discussion of this support. Could you make your point best by analyzing your material in the same order as it appears in the novel? By dealing with all your examples of the "minister's torment" first and then dealing with Hester's fate? By contrasting one illustration of Dimmesdale's "torment" to one example of Hester's suffering, and then following by another matched pair, and so on?

3. Rewrite the essay following the suggestions in the Criticism. Devote approximately equal space to a discussion of how Dimmesdale's appearance "betrays great inner strife"; his "obsession with good and bad"; his reasons for not confessing; the function of these aspects of his character in the novel as a whole.

4. Following the suggestions in the Introduction to Chapter 4, write full-length character sketches of Dimmesdale, Hester, Pearl, and Chillingworth.

2 — MY GRANDFATHER

Never in my life have I known a more honest, sincere, and straightforward man than my grandfather. He acquired these qualities only through hardship and misfortune.

His mother died when he was only a year old, and his stepmother was unconcerned with his welfare. He developed an independent spirit, and his childhood was, for the most part, lonely and pitiful.

Lacking a mother's love, he turned instead to hunting and to the out-of-doors. He loved to run and exercise; he could stand on his head and walk on his hands; he could do back-flips and front-flips in mid-air. But while he was still very young, he developed an infection in one of his ears, and he remained partially deaf for the rest of his life.

Being hard of hearing was certainly a disadvantage for my grandfather, but, at the same time, it was a hidden blessing. It seemed to cut him off from all the vices and deception of the otuside world and it enabled him to appreciate the quiet virtues of life. It instilled in him an everlasting honesty and a truehearted straightforwardness that has never left him. He could look any man straight in the eye and speak with quiet respect and sincerity. He had tasted the hardship of life, and he had learned from it.

In the meantime, my grandfather had grown tall, lean, strong, and quick. He played a lot of baseball, and soon became a pitcher in the minor leagues. He pitched one-hitters and two-hitters and no-hitters, and whenever he won a game, he did exuberant back-flips from the pitcher's mound to the player's bench. But he was never a poor winner nor a poor loser. He had signed a contract with a major league team and was ready to leave for spring training when his arm gave out.

Fate had put an end to a brilliant pitcher in baseball, but it had not put an end to my grandfather's hopes, nor had it lessened his courage or his sincerity. He took up farming, the occupation of his father. He farmed like he played baseball, with robust energy and unsophisticated honesty.

Every fall he hunted squirrels and quail. He could never hear the chirping of squirrels cutting nuts, but he seemed to sense their presence. He knew every bush and every tree in the woods. He hunted for enjoyment, and he hunted for food, but he never hunted for excitement alone.

Today my grandfather is over 80 years old. He is still as thin and healthy as he was 30 years ago; he still farms and he still hunts. Never am I so proud and full of respect for anyone as I am when he takes me hunting. He is still lively and he still loves the out-of-doors. I know that he could not stand slowing his lively pace; I am sure that he would rather die tomorrow than spend a year in a nursing home. But most important of all, he still looks people in the eye when he talks.

CRITICISM

This essay is almost excellent. Let us see why "almost excellent" rather than "excellent". Character sketches, whether long or short, must follow the same basic rules of organization, development, and support as are appropriate to all types of writing. The major weakness in this essay is that, because he ignored some of these basic principles of expository prose, the author raises more questions than he answers.

The essay begins well. The opening lines list the qualities which make the grandfather noteworthy, and generalize about the manner in which these qualities were acquired. These introductory statements focus the reader's attention on the aspects of character which will be stressed in the essay.

The author then begins illustrating these points. Unfortunately, although many vivid details and specific facts are presented, certain key statements are left underdeveloped. Consequently the two most significant events in the grandfather's life are treated casually, while less important facts are stressed.

Consider paragraphs two and three. The death of the grandfather's mother is certainly a misfortune, and one can readily see why his unhappy childhood encouraged an "independent spirit." However, why is this independence manifested in a love of the out-of-doors and athletics? Why, for example, did not the young man turn to a life of crime instead, as do so many youngsters in the same circumstances?

The question is, of course, unanswerable. But nonetheless it is a question which any alert reader would ask, and one which the writer is obliged to discuss. Speculation and analysis are in order here. The writer should have told as much as he knew about this central point in the development of his subject, and then have attempted to account for the situation.

This technique is used in paragraph four and, consequently, the section dealing with the grandfather's deafness and its effects on his life is more satisfactory.

Later in the essay we are told simply that, as he was about to enter the major league, "his arm gave out". His career was destroyed but, for some reason, whatever happened to his arm did not affect his ability to farm and hunt. But precisely **what** happened to his arm? Did he strain his muscles in practice pitching? Did he contract some disease which left his arm weak but serviceable?

Thus, because the author has not given his readers the answers to two very important questions, he has weakened an otherwise well-written and effective essay. He has cheated his readers by interesting them in his subject, but then neglecting to tell them what they really want to know.

Aside from these blemishes, good techniques predominate in the sketch. In most cases the author provides vivid pictures of his subjects and stresses details of his actions which are memorable. Readers remember characters who do "exuberant back-flips from the pitcher's mound to the player's bench" after winning a game. They rapidly forget characters who are simply "happy" when they win.

EXERCISES
Many of the author's statements arouse the reader's curiosity, but do not fulfill his desire for clarification. For example, what precisely does the author mean by the assertion the grandfather farms with "unsophisticated honesty"? By the phrase, "he never hunted for excitement alone"? By saying that "his arm gave out"? Using your own imagination to supply details and explanations, rewrite the theme giving support for every such assertion.

3 — HIGHTROU, LOWTROU, MIDDLETROU
When Stone Age Man first put on a pair of britches, he little realized that he was creating a socio-economic classification system which would prevail for over two thousand years. Observing any large high school in the country today, one readily perceives a direct correlation between the level of a boy's trousers (using his navel as a point of reference) and the level of his motivation, his present attitude towards life, and his future status. All boys of high school age can be thrown into three major categories: the hightrou, the middletrou, and the lowtrou.

The lowtrou is the most easily recognized. The waist of his pants clings sleekly around an area roughly three inches below his umbilicus. He is also enwrapped in a T-shirt which, for all practical purposes, should have been condemned months ago.

The lowtrou is characterized by an almost unimaginable lack of motivation. This "germ" is destined to rise no higher than a blue-collar worker.

He is most commonly surrounded by an aura of luscious "blondes" who would rather go drinking with the boys than go talking about the boys with the girls. These debutantes usually accompany their beaus to the local snack shop: a haven for retired human beings which is so clouded with the smoke of a myriad of white cylindrical tubes that only God knows what transpires in the booths in the back. If any of these "waist" products of society ever decided to peer through the smoke, through the window, and out onto the sidewalk, he would see a young gentleman pass, walking hand-in-hand with one of the nicest looking girls in the whole school. He would, in short, see a middletrou.

The middletrou wears his trousers where Beau Brummell meant them to be worn — on his waist. He is the boy who wouldn't think of buying a sport shirt until he has checked for a rolled collar, a front pleat, and a back pleat.

Being "better" than everyone else, the middletrou finds security in small, closed groups consisting of other such conceited individuals. These groups are commonly termed "cliques". For each of these cliques there is a corresponding girls' group. All such groups are characterized by a hierarchy of authority. Whenever two corresponding groups get together, they are expected to mix, with only the most influential members of the groups actually pairing off.

The middletrou, possessing sufficient motivation to get himself through three or possibly even four years of college, will find his place in our society as a white collar worker.

Moving farther up the scale, we eventually arrive at the individual who will, in time, marry the girl whom the middletrou is dating at the present. This is the hightrou. The hightrou is as style conscious as the lowtrou is motivated. In fact, the only reason he wears a belt is to prevent his pants from falling below his chest. A common misconception is that he is inherently pale. The reason that the hightrou is so pasty is that he spends practically all of his time at his desk.

Although he firmly believes that girls are merely soft boys and that a quarterback is nothing more than a refund, the hightrou will have dissolved these naive attitudes by the time he reaches college. Indeed, he definitely will go to college and most likely to graduate school. His attitudes towards hard work and perseverance, for which he is presently being scoffed at, are the same qualities which will someday get him his Ph.D.

CRITICISM

"Hightrou, Lowtrou, Middletrou" is an example of the essay which uses character sketches as means of making its point rather than because the characters described are of interest in themselves. In spite of certain weaknesses, it is a highly effective essay.

The essay is successful because it is fun to read. Although he describes the commonplace, the author substitutes clever and original synonyms for obvious word choices. The phrases "roughly three inches below his umbilicus" is much more effective — and memorable — than "a few inches below the waist" because it is novel, unexpected, and whimsical.

Note the handling of comedy. Although witty lines are found throughout the essay, we do not find any actual jokes until the concluding sections. If such a pun as the play on the word "quarterback" occurred at the beginning of the essay, we would turn from it in disgust. Since we have been prepared for it by the lighthearted tone of the essay as a whole, however, the joke succeeds.

Certain sections of the essay are much better written than others. The author is at his best when he offers precise descriptions; he is weakest when he avoids details by the use of such meaningless phrases as "a T-shirt which . . . should have been condemned months ago" and "small, closed groups consisting of other such conceited individuals."

Another weakness is the author's tendency to lose his objectivity. He is so clearly partial to the "hightrou" that his attacks on the other types tend to be vicious.

This same prejudice leads him to overlook an obvious point. Each type is very strongly motivated, but the goals of each differ. By "motivation" the author apparently means "intellectual" or "financial" motivation rather than what he says.

EXERCISES

1. Use of the term "motivation" throughout the essay is, at best, ambiguous. How could the meaning which the author intends to convey by use of this word be clarified? Consider the effectiveness

of adding a paragraph clearly defining the sense in which the term is used, the possibility of substituting such phrases as "intellectual motivation" and "goals in life" as various points, or any other means you can think of to clarify the meaning.

2. The author frequently betrays his personal prejudices by the terms he uses. For example, he calls lowtrous "germs" and "retired human beings", and insists that middletrous are conceited. Since objectivity would heighten the overall effectiveness of the essay, study these overly subjective sections and consider ways of saying the same things in less offensive ways.

3. Write a character sketch of the author of this essay accounting for his reasons for regarding his contemporaies as he does.

4. When the author uses concrete terms and vivid descriptions he is at his best; he is weakest when he evades description by using such meaningless phrases as "only God knows what transpires in the booths in the back" and "a T-shirt which, for all practical purposes, should have been condemned months ago." Supply the vivid details which are missing in these "descriptions" and certain others.

5. Add a section illustrating the author's assertion that the middletrou feels he is "better" than everyone else.

6. Compare the humour in this essay to that used in Essay 2-1. Are the techniques similar or different? Do the authors use humour to achieve different, or similar, effects? In which essay does the humour more effectively support the overall purpose of the essay?

CHAPTER 5

CREATIVE WRITING

Everyone likes a good story. We enjoy some stories simply because they entertain us and hold our interest, others because they deepen our insights into life. The best often do both: we are fascinated by what happens, yet come away from the narrative realizing that we have more knowledge or now feel differently than before about something.

Whatever an author's initial inspiration for writing, or whatever his motive for doing so, his narrative must be planned with the reader in mind. Every element in the story — words and phrases as well as scenes and characters — must add to the effect on the reader.

A reader should be able to visualize every detail in a story, and for this reason word choice is a major consideration. It is not enough for you — as an author — to know what *you* mean: you must make your readers see it and feel it as well. Thus, the more specific and concrete your words, the more clear will be the action to the reader.

The meaning of a story — if it has one — must be inherent in the story itself. Never tell your readers the moral of your tale; rather, tell the story in such a way that the "message" is inescapable.

Lastly, never tell more than is necessary to the story itself. The reader has no interest in what your characters do *off-stage*: he takes for granted that they "remain in character" but otherwise do pretty much what everyone else does. Focus his attention on the story; show him how your characters behave in, and react to, the situations which *are* the story; and simply sketch in any necessary background as rapidly and as unobtrusively as possible.

Basic rules of writing aside, let's examine the stories at hand.

The story — "The Obnoxious Brain" — was written primarily to instruct. The author, before writing the story, formulated certain opinions on a subject, and then invented characters and situations to illustrate this thesis. Be sure to keep this point in mind when considering the success of the story.

The second story — "The Trick Was on Them" — was written primarily because the author thought he had a good story to tell. Does it interest you as much as he thought it would?

"Unforgettable Evening" combines both approaches to writing. The author wished to tell a good story as well as share his insights into life with the reader; consequently, it is impossible to tell which element came first — the philosophy, or the story which illustrates it.

Read each story and try to formulate your own opinions about it before turning to our criticisms.

1 — THE OBNOXIOUS BRAIN

Hortense stomped down the hall in her usual manner. Her head was leading while her derriere trailed a few blocks behind, and her duck-like waddle added to the spectacle. During this time, Hortense, oblivious of her own predicament, was imitating the pigeon-toed girl who walked ahead of her. She was having too much fun to answer any greetings which chanced to come her way.

At last she reached her class and entered with a look that said, "Well, here I am, you peasants!" One of her cronies was already in the room. Immediately Hortense began a boisterous discussion of the day's assignment to show everyone that she not only had read Plato's *Republic,* but that she also understood it thoroughly.

The bell rang, and she plopped into her chair. Class discussion began, but Hortense contributed none of the thoughts she had displayed before class. Instead she amused herself by disturbing those around her with remarks she thought were very witty. When Julia Mead, a hard-working girl, asked a question, Hortense replied with a laugh. Julia blushed and said no more for the rest of the period.

The class ended, and Hortense jumped up to brag to her friend how quickly she had completed the assignment. But she neglected to mention that her father had bought her an excellent synopsis of the book which explained all the difficult ideas in it.

As she and her friend were passing through the door, Hortense made some comments about Alice Nelson's appearance. Alice was wearing an outer brace to help straighten her teeth. It made no difference that Hortense had just had her own braces taken off. Nor did she compare her own beak nose and mannish face to Alice's pretty and feminine one.

Hortense now left her friend and began pushing aside those who dared to get in her way as she waddled down the hall. She soon stalked into her next class. A similar scene was about to begin.

CRITICISM

Although similar in many respects to the essays in Chapter 4, "The Obnoxious Brain" is a short story rather than a character sketch. While Hortense is, to some extent, representative of a type (as are the "trous" in Essay 3), she is at the same time unique enough to be atypical (as is the grandfather in Essay 2). Her primary function in the story is to illustrate a truth about life.

In a postscript to the story, the author stated that his purpose was to depict a common human failing: our tendency to overlook our own faults while magnifying the shortcomings of others. Since the story does not accomplish this, it cannot be considered totally successful. Without the author's help, we could only guess at his overall intentions: parts seem designed solely to amuse us, while other sections apparently attempt to evoke our sympathy for Hortense's victims.

The story is ineffective because not all parts lead the reader to the insight desired by the author. Buried in the first and fifth paragraphs are the only clues to the meaning of the story: When we first meet Hortense, she is "oblivious of her own predicament"; later we learn that she has forgotten about her own recently removed braces and is unaware of "her own beak nose and mannish face."

Since the story is about Hortense's blindness to her own defects, these observations should be given more emphasis. Every action should reveal this flaw in Hortense's character. Material for such revelations abound in the story, but the author has neglected to make his incidents work for him.

For example, we do not learn whether or not Hortense herself was aware of the fact that her knowledge of Plato was secondhand, and that she was not, in fact, very smart at all. The meaning of the story would be supported by her inability to see what is obvious to the reader. If, however, she is aware of her stupidity and consciously attempts to cover it up, we are dealing with an aspect of her personality which is unrelated to the *theme* of the story.

The story-telling techniques used by the author are, for the most part, excellent. In most cases he chooses words which permit the reader to visualize precisely what he is describing. Hortense stomps, waddles, and stalks through the hallways; characters in whom we are less interested merely walk. Certain details, however, cannot be visualized: What precisely makes Hortense's face mannish? In what way is Alice Nelson pretty and feminine? The reader should be permitted to decide these things for himself because of details supplied by the author.

EXERCISE

1. Delete all non-descriptive words and substitute terms which permit the reader to see precisely what is going on. For example, describe Alice Nelson's pretty and feminine face and contrast it to a description of Hortense's mannish one.

2. Rewrite each section of the essay which does not reveal Hortense's blindness to her own defects.

3. Could Hortense, ugly and obnoxious as she is, be transformed into a sympathetic character? How would you go about making the reader feel sorry for her? Would this add to, or detract from, the author's purpose in writing the story?

2 — THE TRICK WAS ON THEM

Three girls by the names of Jane, Linda, and Sue were common in many ways. For example, they all came from wealthy families; they all went with boys none of their parents liked; and they all became frightened very easily.

One night when Jane's parents went out, she invited her two friends to stay at her house because then they could go out with their boy friends without letting their parents know about it. The girls were more than willing to come, especially since they liked the idea of fooling their parents.

The boys picked up the three girls and they all went to a movie. When they got out of the movie they went riding around in a car. One of the girls turned on the radio and they heard the announcer tell of a maniac who had escaped from a nearby asylum. He was said to be dangerous and armed with a sharp knife. Of course this news scared the girls and they asked to be taken home immediately because Jane remembered that she didn't lock the house when they left.

Now I have to mention two important factors about this story. First, the door to Jane's bedroom squeaked when opened and, second, Jane had a little poodle that slept alongside of her bed. When she got scared in the night, Jane often dropped her hand over the side of the bed, her dog licked it, and this helped her to overcome her fright.

After the girls returned to the house, they decided that it would be best to check all the rooms. Each was assigned to search a certain part of the house. When they were through, they went to Jane's bedroom and crawled into bed. But, to their dismay, she confessed that she hadn't checked the basement bcause she had been too scared.

Now that they were already in their pajamas and in bed, they agreed that no one would want to go down there. They talked for awhile and soon Sue and Linda fell asleep. But Jane couldn't. Her mind kept wandering down to the basement. She dropped her hand over the side of the bed and felt her dog lick it. As usual, she was reassured.

She felt even more secure after her bedroom door opened and closed, for she was sure that meant her parents had returned home. In spite of this, however, she continued to feel somewhat uneasy, so she kept her hand hanging over the bed. The dog continued to lick it and finally she fell asleep.

When she woke in the morning she looked at her two friends: their throats had been cut. She began to stand up when she noticed that her poodle's throat had also been cut. There was a note on its little body. Written in shaky handwriting, it read, "A man can lick a girl's hand just as well as a dog."

CRITICISM

Anyone who has ever watched a child's reaction to a horror story will immediately perceive the major weaknesses in this tale. It is inherently terrifying, but the author has forgotten his reasons for telling it.

A child knows intuitively how he wants his spooky stories told to him. By continually asking questions about how characters feel when they first hear of the monster who might be lurking in the shadows, by repeatedly requesting clarification of precisely how dark and foggy it was, young auditors slow the progress of the narrative and so prolong their own terror at what will finally happen.

Adults as well as children enjoy horror stories and "monster" shows because they like to be scared. Everyone knows that they are blatantly untrue; we often laugh afterwards at how we had permitted our own emotions to be so manipulated. While enjoying them, however, we consciously "suspend disbelief" in order to experience their full effect on us.

Thus horror stories are either good or bad depending upon how well they entertain us. And since they entertain for only so long as they last, the final agony should be continually anticipated, but reached only after the reader has been scared out of his wits.

In outline, "The Trick Was On Them" is a classic horror story. Ever since the time of Aristotle, the narrative pattern of the character who suffers as a direct consequence of his own actions has been recognized as the most satisfying. Here the characters consciously break two rules: they disobey their parents and they choose to ignore whatever dangers may be lurking in the basement. The outcome of the story is a result of these choices.

In addition, there are few loose ends in the narrative. Most details invented by the author — from turning on the car radio to the habits of Jane's dog — have a function in the story. Only a little of the information presented in the first three paragraphs is unnecessary, or at least capable of compression.

The story does not succeed, however, because it is poorly told in terms of what it is designed to accomplish. The reader should be made to feel the impending horror from the moment he begins the story; fear for the characters and terror at what is unknown to them — yet expected by us — should increase with every line.

Such effects could have been achieved by the author if he had told his story more leisurely, filling out every description and incident with details designed to scare the reader. For example, the emotions of the reader would have been properly manipulated had he peered into the darkened rooms along with the girls, and had he been told in more detail how frightened each was — too frightened, perhaps, to recognize clues to the intruder's presence which the reader, of course, would have seen.

A second fault of the story is that the author draws attention to the fact that it is *merely* a story in paragraph four. We all know that it is fiction, but prefer to believe — while reading it — that perhaps, just perhaps, all this really might have happened.

EXERCISES

1. The story contains a good deal of careless wording. The first sentence is perhaps the very worst in the story. The author seems to be saying that these were common — that is, cheap — girls, whereas he means, of course, that they had many things in *common*. Rewrite any individual sentence which does not say precisely what you know (or suspect) the author means.

2. A fundamental rule in writing fiction is to introduce necessary information casually, without drawing attention to the fact that the information is necessary to the story. Introduce the two "important factors" of paragraph four into the story more smoothly. Be sure to consider the effect these factors will create, and place them so as to achieve the greatest "spooky" effect on the reader with them.

3. Any narrative should be constructed of individual scenes that the reader can visualize, connected by passages which, while supplying necessary information, do not impede the progress of the story with nonessential details. Construct an outline of this story, listing the important scenes which the reader should see to gain the full effect.

4. The story is told partly from the omniscient point of view (where the author tells us everything we should know) and partly from the third person point of view (when we see everything only through Jane's eyes and mind). It is usually most effective to be consistent throughout, for then the reader most readily identifies

himself with the person from whose perspective the story is told. Can you find any justification for the shift in point of view in this story? If not, consider telling the story entirely from the omniscient point of view, and again from Jane's point of view. Which would be more effective? Why?

5. The title is inappropriate, for it gives the reader no clue to what kind of story he is about to read. Can you think of a better one?

UNFORGETTABLE EVENING

Gabe Bishop was a seventeen-year-old girl when I first met her. It was a meeting of mixed emotions for me. I was just an average student in an average high school in an average town. I wasn't a mighty basketball player or a husky football fullback. I played golf, yet I never had much of a girl problem. I went steady my senior year until the night of the Prom.

She was standing against the wall at the biggest dance of the year when we arrived. My steady and I went through the reception line, and before I knew it, we were just inches away from her. We were all laughing and having a fine time, but she was alone.

Her eyes were shut and a smile curved her lips. It didn't bother her to be alone, and suddenly so was I. Barb was dancing with Dave Robbins. I was mad, I can tell you! With a snort I sat down in a nearby chair. It was then she spoke to me.

"Who is sitting there? What boy is it?"

"How did you know it was a boy who sat down here?"

"I smell your Jade East." She turned and faced me. "What's your name?"

"I'm Thor Davidson."

"Why, then you're my brother's friend. He's Bob Bishop."

I was surprised and stood up. "I didn't even know Bob had a sister. How come you aren't around more?" I could have bitten my tongue when I said that, because as I stood facing her I realized what made her so different. She was blind.

"I go to a school for the blind," she told me. Suddenly she turned her head slightly, listened for a moment, and then announced that her brother was approaching them.

I was stunned. I sent a silent message towards Heaven asking the Lord how he could make someone as lovely as she blind.

Bob walked up to us and put his arm affectionately around his sister's waist. "I see you've met Gabrielle."

"Gabrielle? So that's your name", I said, trying to disguise my confusion by conversation.

Bob chatted away for a few minutes about our missing girl friends — his steady had also deserted him — while Gabe smiled sightlessly in his direction. Suddenly her sightless eyes glittered with excitement, and flushing slightly, she brought her lips close to her brother's face and half-whispered a question to him.

"Bob, tell me, what does Thor look like?"

My friend whooped with delight at the opportunity he was given. "He's a skinny ugly galoot with spaces between his teeth and straw hair that sticks up in all the wrong places. His eyes are as blue as a muddy river bottom and . . ."

She begged him to stop, her face turning crimson. I couldn't tell whether she was delighted by his humour or embarrassed at the humiliation she had brought upon me.

"Well, now that you know the worst," I said, "will you dance with me anyway?"

She seemed confused, but said yes. I led her to the floor and guided her among the other couples. She made me feel like a man who must protect a weak, frail creature. We danced often, and talked for hours about anything and everything. I was so entranced by her that Barb seemed a total stranger when she came up to us on the dance floor and announced that she was going home with Dave if I was too busy to take her myself.

I mumbled something like, "that's nice", hardly bothering to even look at her. I learned later that she and Dave left for an hour or so, and then returned. She put my pin and a ring I had given her into a crumpled handkerchief and left it with Bob for me. I probably thanked him when he gave it to me, but I don't actually remember doing so. All I remember about that night was Gabe, Gabe, Gabe. We had the universe in our hands.

Bob was on the clean-up committee, so I took his sister home. It was then that she told me how she was blinded.

"It was four years ago", she said. "When the time came to move away from our old home to this town, I was determined not to come. I threw temper tantrums and had crying fits. I did everything I could to delay our departure, but nothing worked. The afternoon they took the furniture out of our old house I purposely got in everybody's way and made a big pest of myself. While I was teasing one of the movers, his hands slipped and the crate he was carrying fell on top of me. He was the last person I ever saw."

"How awful for you."

"No, Thor, on the contrary. I was the biggest brat you ever saw before that happened. It was the best thing that ever happened to me. It gave me an insight into myself, even if it destroyed my eyes, I never really cried after I learned I would never see again. I was happy to be alive. I still am."

She said this with such conviction that I stopped feeling sorry for her. It was true: she had some kind of insight or perception that neither I nor anyone I know possessed. Her life had not been ruined by the accident. I silently made my peace with the Lord, for I no longer thought him so harsh.

That night was the only time I saw her until years later when, just beginning graduate work at a college away from my hometown, I walked into a classroom for the first time and discovered that she would be my professor. Although an expert in her field, I saw during her first lecture that she hadn't changed. Gabe still glowed with the light of inner peace. She knew me immediately when I walked up to her after class.

"Hello, Thor", she said.

"How did you know it was me?" I hadn't said a word.

"We spent an evening together, years ago. I remember your walk."

Details of that Prom night came back to me with a rush. "And I'm not even wearing *Jade East*", I said. She smiled with pleasure that I remembered our meeting so vividly.

"I can never forget that night", she said. She blushed suddenly as if she wished she hadn't said that. She turned away from me and began fumbling for some books on the desk. "You'll be late for your next class", she said. "I can manage by myself."

Now that I had found her again, I didn't intend to be dismissed so easily, even if she was my teacher. "But I'd like to help you", I told her. "And, really, I have absolutely nothing better to do. . ."

We were married the following fall. Perhaps we weren't wise in doing so, for I depend too much on my small blind wife. She has never seen our children, and she never will, yet I know that the kids

60

are growing up thinking that sight is unimportant, but that the love of the Almighty and His infinite mercy and good judgment is.

CRITICISM

"Unforgettable Evening" is, on the whole, an excellent story, although its effect is weakened by some minor blemishes.

Its worst fault is the final line. Here the author attempts to impose a meaning upon the story which the story itself does not reveal. The most effective ending would have been the next to last paragraph, for the narrator's final line implies the relationship which will continue after the story itself ends.

The dialogue is good because it imitates the speech patterns of real people; descriptions are effective because the author permits his readers to visualize most details. The major stylistic weakness is the author's occasional use of meaningless and non-vivid phrases, such as "We had the universe in our hands".

Finally, the story is effective because the author focuses his reader's attention on two central characters, and ignores all non-essentials. Five or six years are passed over in a dependent clause; all we hear of Thor's "steady" is what relates to our understanding of his relationship with Gabe.

EXERCISES

1. We are never told what any of the characters actually look like. Is this an oversight of the author's or is it intentional? Describe Thor and Gabe in a paragraph for each, and then compare your descriptions with those of others in the class. Would the story be more or less effective if the most apt descriptions were worked into it? Why?

2. Describe the emotions and motivations of Barb, and account for her behaviour after leaving the Prom with Dave. Has the author of "Unforgettable Evening" given you enough information to permit you to reach any conclusions about Barb?

3. Why does Gabe blush at the end of the story "as if she wished she hadn't said" what she did? Should the author have told you explicitly what Thor thought went through her mind at that moment?

4. A reader should always be able to visualize the settings in which he finds the characters. List the individual scenes in the story, and find any details which describe the setting. The background for one major scene is not even suggested. Which? Add appropriate details as necessary.

CHAPTER 6
THE BOOK REPORT

Many students think that book reports should be, primarily, summaries of the works they have read. Such is not the case at all. A report should draw the reader's attention to some of the most significant aspects of the book; it should permit him to decide whether or not the book holds any interest for him.

If you stop to think about it, you'll find that the major interest in most good books does not lie at all in the stories they tell. In any case, if all that one cared about were the plot of a book, your report could never be a substitute for a firsthand reading of the work.

Therefore, when asked to write a book report, try to find the essence of the work and organize your essay around this. A good way to begin is to ask yourself precisely why you reacted to the book as you did. If you admired certain characters and disliked others, perhaps the way in which the author described them is the key to enjoyment of the work.

If, on the other hand, the moral or philosophy presented interested you, you might organize your report around a discussion of this. Another possibility is that you found yourself completely confused by the work. In such a case you might build your report around the difficulties the book presents to the reader.

Yet another possibility is to speculate in your report as to why the author wrote the book as he did. Your statements about the plot, characters, and style would then be used as illustrations of what he did, and as support for your opinions as to why he did it.

The other elements of a comprehensive book report should be subordinate to the focus of your essay. If, for example, you mention the author, say no more about him than is relevant to helping your readers appraise the book.

Your recommendations are often better implied than explicitly stated. It is seldom necessary for you to say that you liked or disliked the book, or that you think the readers of your report might enjoy it. The words you choose in discussing the book will usually betray — as they should — your attitude towards it, and your readers — independent thinkers all — will resent your telling them what to do.

Most important, however, remember that no one likes to know how a story turns out until he has had the pleasure of reading it for himself. When discussing the plot of a novel or story, do no more than tell your readers very sketchily what the work is about. To give the plot away is to deprive your readers of any suspense they might experience while reading it for themselves.

1 — JENNIE GERHARDT BY THEODORE DREISER

Jennie Gerhardt was a very beautiful but naive girl. She did not have much schooling. She fell in love with a senator who died before he had married her. This senator was very much older than Jennie. He had had much experience in his lifetime where Jennie had had none. Jennie's mother was very sympathetic and helpful. She always stuck up for Jennie, but Jennie's father was just the opposite. Her brothers and sisters were very close. Later, after the senator died, she found another man. This man was a man of very high society. His father owns a carriage company. He will not marry Jennie but he wants her to live with him anyway.

The people in this book were different from the people nowadays. They were less educated but they stuck together more than the family does today.

The character which I liked was Jennie because she was so sweet and innocent and never complained or gave anyone a hard time in her time of trouble. She was very understanding. Also I liked seeing someone grow up in so very short a time.

The author's purpose was to show how one can be beaten by the forces of life. This book was written to teach some moral lessons. His success was very well accomplished because his lessons stand out well in my mind.

In the above paragraph I stated that his lessons stood out well in my mind. What I mean is that his book has explained many moral lessons to me which were a little foggy to me before.

The story on the whole was very touching. It never left you in suspense.

I would recommend this book because it has a few deep concepts that are the main points of the story. If you don't understand those, there is no sense in even going on to finish the book.

CRITICISM

This report is totally unsatisfactory. The author does little more than retell the basic story very poorly. He says he "liked" Jennie, found the book "touching", and would recommend it. However, he gives absolutely no reasons why his readers should accept any of his judgments.

The story is summarized inadequately and unwisely. Minor incidents are given equal weight with the major themes, and there is very little continuity. Interpretations, such as the author's assertions that Jennie's mother was "sympathetic and helpful", that her father was "just the opposite", and that her siblings were "very close", are not supported by references to the text, but are treated like the facts of the story which surround them.

Evaluations in the report ("the people in this book were different from the people nowadays"; "the author's purpose was to show how one can be beaten by the forces of life") are equally unsupported and unsubstantiated.

Perhaps the worst fault of the report is the author's references to the "moral lessons" in the book. Precisely what these are is never mentioned, yet three paragraphs are devoted to them. And, clearly, one suspects that the author of the report is overrating his comprehension of the novel in paragraph five.

In short, the report is a failure because it says nothing of any value, and, in spite of the author's protestations to the contrary, makes Jennie seem a very dull girl.

EXERCISES

1. Write a short essay in which you analyze and characterize the style of paragraph one. Comment on (a) the variation, or lack of it, in sentence patterns; (b) subordination of material; (c) repetition, intentional or otherwise; (d) use of punctuation; (e) transitions between sentences; (f) sentence rhythm; (g) logical paragraph development; and (h) the overall effectiveness of the paragraph. Your discussion should pinpoint many of the characteristics of immature writing.

2. Instead of exercise one, rewrite the paragraph in a polished and mature style. Alter the content as necessary.

3. List the clichés you find in this essay.

4. Underline the colloquial diction in the theme. Why is it out of place in a formal essay?

5. Outline the points which the author makes which, if properly expanded and developed, might serve a worthwhile function in a book report.

6. Find and correct the tense shift in paragraph one. (Note that shifts of this type occur because an author is thumbing through

a book while actually writing his essay, and consequently fails to see his own words objectively.)

7. The author's favourite word appears to be "very" for he uses it eight times in the essay. Seldom does the word convey the exact meaning intended. For example, just how much older is the senator in sentence four? A man five years older than a girl fourteen is "very" much older, but so is a man of fifty-five years older. Find more precise terms for each of these eight vague "very's".

8. In paragraph 6 the author of the essay states that the story "never left you in suspense". This is obviously untrue, for a reader is always in suspense until he finishes a story and learns what happens. Explain what the author means, but does not say, in this sentence.

9. As pointed out in the Criticism, the author never tells you what he means by the "moral lessons" and "deep concepts" he mentions so often. Assume for the moment that the essay contained one paragraph describing these points. How, then, could the essay be reorganized into a logical and effective presentation of the essence of the novel?

2 — THE AGONY AND THE ECSTASY BY IRVING STONE

Irving Stone, a twentieth century novelist, has made his talent known with the publication of his biographical novel, *The Agony and the Ecstasy*. Author of another book, *Lust for Life,* Stone is remembered for his moving narrative of the life of the great Renaissance painter and sculptor, Michelangelo Buonarroti. Although this masterpiece cannot be considered nonfiction, much of the book is based on actual facts compiled after years of research in the areas of Europe in which Michelangelo lived and worked.

The purpose of this book is certainly to create a detailed *description* of the life of the famous Michelangelo.

Stone starts his moving novel when Michelangelo is a mere boy of thirteen years. The author delves deeply into the mind and feelings of this adolescent who is to become one of the world's most renowned artists. As is normal, the boy's feelings and ideas become more and more complex as he grows into manhood.

Through Stone's excellent descriptions, the reader begins seeing the palace of the wealthy Medici family and, in contrast, the home of *his* somewhat unhappy family. You will become well acquainted with his friends and enemies alike. Every thought that occurs to the young Michelangelo is written in such a way that the book becomes very flowing. As the boy grows, so do his loves, fears, joys, and more important, his talent. His successful so-called "apprenticeship" to the great Bertoldo gave Michelangelo a great experience and brought him in contact with his first love, the contessina, the beautiful daughter of the powerful Lorenzo d'Medici. After the death of his master and later of Lorenzo, Michelangelo begins travelling and soon comes in contact with his second love. His talent becomes more firmly established with the years. While in Rome, Bologna, and other parts of southern Italy, he completes sculptures which will later place him among the great artists of all times.

While fulfilling his main purpose of portraying the life of Michelangelo, Stone also incorporates into the story an excellent description of this great age in world history.

Irving Stone carried out his purpose in a way equalled by few writers. His vivid accounts give the book a realistic tone which holds the reader's interest throughout.

I found this book interesting and would recommend it to anyone who enjoys reading for pleasure and facts.

CRITICISM

The essay is better focused than the first and consequently leads the reader to a better understanding of what he might expect to find in the novel. A good portion of what the author has to say about the book is presented in terms of the factual manner in which Stone treated his subject. The essay is weakest, however, when the author neglects to subordinate his material to basic focus.

Emphasized in both the first and final paragraphs is the point that Stone based his novel on fact. Since this is the basis of the author's terming it a "masterpiece" and recommending it to his readers, he is obligated to show in some detail what this element adds to the novel. Yet none of the three paragraphs which summarize the story so much as suggests which features of the book are based on fact, and which on speculation.

For example, it is unlikely that Stone was able to find facts which supported his delving "deeply into the mind and feelings of this adolescent." His analysis of the emotions of his subject might have been inferred from factual data, or it may be sheer invention on Stone's part. The author of the essay, since he so stresses the factual substrata of the novel, must clarify such matters for his readers.

Another weakness of the essay is that, although the flow of prose is smooth, very often the words used by the author are so imprecise as to be meaningless. He calls the novel "moving," Stone's descriptions "excellent", and the homelife of Michelangelo "somewhat happy", but since no illustrations of what these adjectives mean is offered, the reader can only guess. He must wonder if the terms connote the same to the author of the essay as to himself.

The opening paragraph is extremely poor. Only if the reader knows the subject matter of each of the novels before he reads this report can he determine which book deals with the Renaissance.

EXERCISES

1. Rewrite paragraph one, clarifying which novel is the subject of the report, and eliminating all the author says that is irrelevant to the novel under consideration.

2. To what extent does paragraph three require additional support? What statements or implications are unexplained?

3. Point out additional statements in the essay which lack adequate support. If you are familiar with the novel, what support could you offer for them?

4. What is the grammatical antecedent of "his" in the first sentence of paragraph four? Rewrite, eliminating the ambiguity.

5. Does the author's use of the phrase "so-called 'apprenticeship' " in paragraph four hinder or aid his attempt to tell his readers about the novel? Why?

3 — EXPERIMENT IN LIVING

Walden, by Henry David Thoreau, is a true-to-life account of two years spent in solitude and contemplation of nature. The author, fearing that his daily life lacked the meaning intended by his Creator, withdrew to a rude cabin on the shore of Walden Pond, near Concord, Massachusetts, in the summer of 1845. Here, to challenge the accepted ideas of mankind, he set down his experiences and realizations in the form of *Walden.*

Thoreau's feelings toward everything from schooling to journalism invade the pages of the book to unveil new vistas of appreciation to the reader. New twists on old trains of thought constantly amaze Thoreau's audience, and one finds himself painting his everyday world in new, exciting colours. Considering the idea that all men are not fully awake to the joys of living makes one observe his surroundings with new comprehension. A school which presents to its students the problems of everyday life instead of the problems of solid geometry teases the reader's imagination. Thoreau's conclusion that simplification is the key to the solution of the complexity of everyday problems makes one pause and survey his own demanding schedule.

Walden, by Henry David Thoreau, is a study of nature in his most glorious attire and life at its highest level. The author's magnificent descriptions captivate his readers, and the timelessness of Thoreau's command to "Simplify! Simplify!" grips one with its fitness. The book is thoughtfully written and expresses the ideas of a man who believes that he has found the key to a true appreciation of life. Thoreau's experiment in living fills the reader with a sudden urge to discover his own personal *Walden.*

CRITICISM

This essay is the most successful of the three book reports because all the material presented has been subordinated to the author's purpose of informing his readers about the essence of *Walden.*

Different in approach from the preceding reports, this might best be termed an "impressionistic" handling of the assignment. The author describes what he found in the book by telling his readers what it meant to him personally. The method is effective insofar as the author is able to imply that his readers will react to the work in the same way.

The essay, however, is far from perfect. One weakness is the author's apparent uncritical acceptance of all he found in *Walden.* While condemnation of a book — or even a part of one — simply to appear perceptive is a distortion of truth, lack of restraint in praise tends to make one sound more like a salesman than an objective critic.

In addition, the author sometimes rhapsodizes at the expense of meaning. "Nature in his most glorious attire" (an unorthodox choice of gender!) could refer to the various beauties found in nature during the different seasons, or solely to the way the woods appear in summer when all is in full bloom, or, just as likely, as the skins of various animals.

EXERCISES

1. The second and third paragraphs are filled with phrases noting the effects of the book on the reader. Would the essay be as

effective if some of these phrases were deleted, and if the author did not emphasize so often such effects?

2. Do you consider the author's beginning both the first and third paragraph with precisely the same phrase effective?

3. Explain the meaning of the word "rude" in paragraph one. Is this a good word choice? Why?

4. Is the author's use of the title "Experiment in Living" appropriate to what he has to say in the essay? Would you (assuming you had some choice in the matter) be more inclined to read the essay if it were entitled "Walden"?

CHAPTER 7

LITERARY CRITICISM

A literary critic does not — as is often assumed — merely point out weaknesses in literature. Rather, his job is to elucidate, explain, and evaluate. Admittedly, if a work does not accomplish its author's purpose, or if its philosophy disagrees with the critic's, the critic is free to say so. But all his comments must be the result of careful study of the work, and he must prove all that he says.

The critic who relies solely on condescending phrases and clever invective convinces his readers of nothing. "Critical" essays by such authors are best regarded as unintentional character sketches of themselves — persons too blind to recognize their own limitations.

A true critical essay has very little in common with a book report. While both, because of their subject matter, either attract readers to the work under discussion or repel them, the report is concerned with broad outlines and essences, while the critical paper deals with subtleties of which the general reader is unaware.

The book report, then, talks about what the author of the literature examined has written; the critical essay deals with his reasons for writing it as he did.

Perhaps the best approach to the critical assignment is to think of the book to be analyzed as a collection of facts about which you must express an opinion. Whatever you say must, of course, be amply supported by references to these "facts". You must be objective enough about your own reactions to the work to express opinions which are of interest to readers of literature. No one wants to hear of your personal prejudices or watch you reveal your blind spots;

readers are interested, however, in your maturely considered, well-expressed evaluations.

In addition, remember that the content of a book is of little interest to the reader of a critical paper; he is concerned with what you, as a critic, have to say *about* the book.

Always assume that your reader is thoroughly familiar with the work you are discussing, and never waste time on summaries of the plot or long quotations from the text. Refer as briefly and succinctly to the elements of the work as required to make your points comprehensible: your reader will go back to the original work himself if he must refresh his memory about it.

1 — IDEALS?

Henry David Thoreau's philosophy in *Walden* is an odd one. He goes to Walden to do an experiment to prove — what? He says he is going to the woods "because I wished to live deliberately, to front only the essential facts of life." All right, so he proved it and liked it, but why did he leave after it was over?

While he was there he proved that the things we call necessities are really only luxury and that making friends with a tree or flowers is the same or better than making it with a friend, though he admits that you need love and understanding from human sources. He goes beyond reality sometimes and into the heart with his thoughts and ideas. His ideas, to the people of America, are considered absurd to some, but to others who understand him, they realize there is great thought in them, but that they are not men and women enough to act upon them.

I believe there are many flaws in Thoreau's ideas. He thinks you can't be free, that is completely free, if you really love someone and I do not think that you can love someone and not be dependent upon him or her in some way or you really don't love them. A person can feel pity or sorrow for a person and still be independent. I think that if you are going to concentrate so hard on being independent and forget about society and friends, then the ideals are lost.

I really do believe that Thoreau's ideas in some respects are good and should be considered, but then again with ideas like these interpreted in the wrong way, you could start another government and end up with ideal like Marx and Stalin and Lenin. So I think even Thoreau isn't sure about which of the things he says are just talk, and the ideas which should be practiced in reserve, if practiced at all.

CRITICISM

This paper was returned to the student with the following comment from his instructor: "I'm sorry, John, but *what* in heaven's name are you trying to say? None of this paper makes *any* sense!"

Such, of course, is the only possible reaction a reader could have to this essay. While at first glance it might appear that mechanics and diction are responsible for its utter incomprehensibility, closer analysis reveals a more fundamental problem.

The author obviously did not agree with the philosophy of *Walden*. Instead of taking the time to analyze the reasons for this disagreement, however, he childishly scribbled some disconnected ideas about it without really thinking about what he was saying. By so doing he merely revealed his own inability to understand Thoreau for, certainly, none of the points are valid.

What should a student do if he finds himself hating a piece of literature so violently that he cannot muster enough objectivity to discuss it coherently in an assigned essay? And what of the student who is man enough to admit to himself that he simply does not understand a book he has been asked to criticize?

One possibility is to write a essay showing that such a reaction to the work is justified. The style of the original, for example, may be so antiquated that a contemporary reader would be unable to understand what the author meant. Or, perhaps the philosophy of the work is so complex that the general reader requires additional background study before he can properly evaluate it.

Had the author of this essay discussed the reasons for his reaction to *Walden* along one of these suggested lines instead of letting his spleen control his mind, he might have produced a worthwhile critical essay.

Mechanical problems will be discussed in the Exercise section.

EXERCISES

A. *Paragraph One*

1. Why does the phrase "an odd one" sound so awkward? Why is "odd" such a poor choice of word in the context of the first sentence? Rewrite the sentence smoothly.

2. Sentence one focuses on Thoreau's philosophy and suggests that the paper will discuss why it is "odd" — whatever that means. How could sentence two begin so as to maintain the focus on Thoreau's philosophy?

3. Why are the various forms of the verb "to go" poor choices for sentences two and three? Find substitutes.

4. Should the author explain what Walden is in sentence two? Why? If so, add a few explanatory words.

5. What element is poor in the phrase "to do an experiment"?

6. What does the author mean to imply or ask by the word "what" which ends sentence two?

7. Find pronoun(s) without clear antecedents in paragraph one. Correct.

8. Why is the concluding sentence poor when considered in relation to what sentence one implied the author was going to talk about?

9. After completing the exercises for paragraph two, write a sentence which makes a good transition between the first and second paragraphs.

B. *Paragraph Two*

10. Find and correct the faulty pronoun or pronouns in sentence one.

11. Why is the word "friend" in the phrase "making it with a friend" a poor word choice in the context of the first sentence?

12. Explain why sentence one is unfocused.

13. Sentence two implies that matters within the heart are "beyond reality". Is this logical? This sentence *may* appear sensible — even profound — if read hastily, but what, precisely, does the author mean?

14. Locate the ambiguous pronoun references in the last sentence. Correct.

15. Where is the phrasing of the final sentence redundant?

C. *Paragraph Three*

16. Explain in detail what parts of this paragraph are unclear in content. Tell why in each case. Consider focus, subordination, development of central ideas, etc., in individual sentences as well as in the paragraph as a whole.

D. *Paragraph Four*

17. The first sentence is poor because the author has not adequately discussed Thoreau's ideas in the preceding paragraphs. Disregarding this weakness, however, study the diction in the first sentence. Rewrite, polishing the phrasing.

18. Explain what phrases and constructions in the final sentence are ungrammatical. Why? Which ideas are illogically expressed? Why?

19. Note that the author uses "you" several times in the essay. Why is this confusing to the reader, and inappropriate in a critical essay?

2 — THOREAU

Thoreau's philosophy of life is, in most respects, very different from other people's philosophies. He believed, as did Emerson, in self-reliance and individualism. In order to find "the essential facts of life", he lived for a period of two years at Walden Pond.

The fact must be emphasized that Walden Pond was almost completely removed from society. It was here that Thoreau found that life could be wonderful. He believed that men should stop wasting their time on trivial matters, and think about more important matters.

"Our life is frittered away by detail. An honest man has hardly need to count more than his ten fingers, or in extreme cases he may add his ten toes, and lump the rest. Simplicity, simplicity, simplicity!"

Thoreau repeats this often in *Walden*. I think that he wants us to honestly examine our souls for the kind of life that we would truly enjoy living. He believed that even though this is a so-called free country, a man would never be completely free unless he stuck up for what he believed in. After all, how could one be free if he didn't have enough courage to defend his beliefs! He certainly wouldn't be free from fear . . . the fear of speaking out.

Thoreau also believed that one should not be dependent on his friends. He should be an individual, doing the things he does because he wants to do them, not because he wants to keep peace with society. Thoreau thought that one shouldn't waste time being sympathetic and loving to other people.

I don't think that one would really be "living" without giving and receiving love. One can't go through life ignoring the hurts of other people and still live a happy life. After all, no one who has any heart at all, can shrug off the death of any person without feeling at least slightly sympathetic. If all the people in this world would use Thoreau's philosophy, this would be an ugly world indeed. How could anyone be happy in such a society? How could anyone enjoy living in such an ugly world of self-concern? What about all the other human beings on this earth who can't take care of themselves; should they just be left to fade away, leaving the "fittest" to rule the world? No! Because the so-called fittest who would be left would not be worthy of continuing the human race, for the simple reason that they would be like animals. Animals live for themselves only. The only way one can truly be living and to enjoy life is to love and be loved; and the only way this is done is to sacrifice, sacrifice, sacrifice!

CRITICISM

This paper, while far superior to the preceding, is not altogether successful. It contains all the elements of a fine critical paper, but does not present them effectively.

The opening sentence is very weak. While it hints at the general subject of the paper, it is too general a statement to focus attention on the central concern of the essay. Instead of vaguely noting that Thoreau's philosophy is "very different from other people's", it should foreshadow the conclusion of the essay which is that the philosophy is inadequate.

The reference to Emerson, while true, has no bearing whatever on the essay. It appears to be an example of a student showing off his knowledge for no reason.

From this point until the final paragraph the author, in somewhat jumbled sequence, summarizes Thoreau's philosophy, tells of his life at Walden, and discusses his purposes in writing. Since these three topics are closely interrelated, they certainly belong in the essay. However, the author has ignored the relationships between the topics, and it is these relationships which are the keys to Thoreau's philosophy.

It is because Walden was isolated that Thoreau recognized the importance of self-reliance and individualism. By living according to his philosophy away from society, he found that "life could be wonderful." (He, of course, expressed this opinion more effectively than did the author of this essay.)

Finally, Thoreau told us of Walden to enable us to share in the pleasure his philosophy brought to him. All this is implied by the author of the essay, but because each paragraph is not focused around one aspect of the total, his presentation does not lead the reader to a clear understanding of the individual points made.

The final paragraph is forcefully written and effective when the author does not permit his impassioned eloquence to lead him into unsupported generalizations. The "fittest" he mentions, for example, are entirely different beings from those who would be produced by Thoreau's philosophy, as any reader of *Walden* knows.

EXERCISES

1. The paragraph development of this essay is poor. In many cases the author uses two paragraphs when one would be more effective; at other times he includes sentences in one paragraph which logically and rhetorically belong in another. Examine the first three paragraphs sentence by sentence and rearrange the material into as many paragraphs as necessary. A few may contain only one sentence. This, of course, indicates that the idea is not fully developed, discussed, or illustrated.

2. In sentences two and three, the author mentions "self-reliance and individualism" and "the essential facts of life". Are these synonymous? If so, clarify and indicate the relationship. If not, distinguish which details and illustrations in the essay apply to each.

3. The first sentence of paragraph two does not emphasize what the author wishes, in spite of what he says. Why does the sentence detract from his meaning? Rewrite.

4. Paragraph two contains several overly general and unsupported terms. How could you clarify the meaning of such phrases as "life could be wonderful", "trivial matters", and "more important matters"? If you have read *Walden,* find specific illustrations from the book. If not, illustrate the terms from your own experience.

5. The antecedent of "this" at the beginning of paragraph four is unclear. Does it refer to the entire quote, or simply to the final three words of the quote? Clarify.

6. Is the repetition of "free" and of "fear" effective or careless in paragraph four? Why?

7. Is the final paragraph a discussion of Thoreau's philosophy or of one aspect of philosophy in general? Introduce the paragraph so as to indicate its proper function in, and relevance to, the entire essay.

3 — MOBY DICK: AN AUTHOR'S EXAMINATION OF ACCEPTED VALUES

From the earliest beginnings of our Judaeo-Christian culture, a primary concern of the religious seems to have been to discern the good from the evil. Even in our novels we of the modern western world expect to find this separation of villain and hero, whether through characters or ideas. With this thought in mind, we find a novel such as Herman Melville's *Moby Dick* somewhat revolutionary. Although every character in the book has some fault, there is none who is completely evil.

At the beginning of the tale we might assume that Melville's purpose is to define evil, but in the course of the novel he presents definitions so contradictory to accepted standards that he leaves his readers wondering if the concept can be categorized at all.

By Christian standards the pagan is one of the lowest forms of humanity. In the first few chapters of *Moby Dick,* Melville makes it clear that he regards this Puritanic evaluation as pure prejudice. *Moby Dick's* narrator, Ishmael, illustrates this opinion by ignoring Christian sailors and choosing for his most intimate friend the cannibalistic idolater, Queequeg.

Through Queequeg's oral autobiography, in which he states that the Christian world has "unfitted him" for his pure pagan life, Melville points out that no way of life is perfect and that this imperfection forms a brotherhood in itself. And when Ishmael states that "Christian kindness has proved but hollow courtesy", but that there are in Queequeg "no civilized hypocrises and bland deceits", we cannot doubt Melville's scorn of "civilized" snobbery. In fact, like Ishmael, Melville seems to believe that sometimes, in a gesture of friendship, all men "must turn idolater".

Certainly, it would seem we might condemn Queequeg for his obvious sin of cannibalism, but Melville does not denounce him on this account. "Who is not a cannibal?" he asks. And when we review the evidence he supplies, it appears that our "cannibalism" compares admirably with that of Queequeg.

Feeling that nature provides as much kinship as a species, Melville concludes that the eating of any animal is most likely as brutal as eating one's own kind of animal. This assumption leads Melville to deride Stubb as he devours his whale steak, Ahab as he consumes his own soul, and the whole of humanity in general. In recognizing evil we find Melville is not content to confine himself to one character but uncovers all the evils of the universe.

When Moby Dick is first mentioned on the Pequod, we instictively hate him for his brutal attack on Ahab. In a purblind defense of the wronged captain, we tend to designate Moby Dick as the only monster in Melville's novel. But after we are given another glimpse at Ahab and his uncontrollable monomania, and at his crew as it mercilessly slaughters the crippled whale, we doubt again the sacredness of men. Like Starbuck, we wonder at this "vengeance on a dumb brute". Perhaps Moby Dick possesses through this inborn mental inferiority an ageless immunity to evil and, in his agelessness, perhaps he becomes symbolic of God.

Having thoroughly confused the subject of the nature of Moby Dick, we are forced to examine that of Ahab. It seems that since the two comprise the major opposing forces of the book, that the character of Ahab controls that of Moby Dick. Melville has refused to allow his characters' souls to be discussed so simply. Although Ahab has his wicked characteristics, he often commands sympathy merely by being human. We cannot deny the sinfulness of Ahab's mad self-destruction, but we must agree with him as he reflects on the "mystic significance" of "all heart woes". Ahab, then, is also neither good nor evil, but man in deepest depression. He is not oppressed by Ishmael's "damp, drizzly November", but by a lifelong tragic obsession.

Discovering the moral message, then, of *Moby Dick* becomes somewhat difficult. Melville is evidently objecting to accepted values, but he has not made his own concept of wickedness as definite as his readers would prefer. Perhaps we come closest to Melville's basic philosophy in the chapter, "The Whiteness of the Whale," in which he points out that white, although symbolic of purity, can become terrifying in many instances. Evil, Melville seems to be saying, is a reality, but it can neither be completely defined nor confined to one individual. It is present in all men, pervades all aspects of life. And life, we find implied in *Moby Dick,* is not contained simply and in its entirety in each human being. We cannot separate each word, each thought, or each person of this world into categories marked "good" and "evil". We are all a mixture of complexities, each of us a combination of good and evil; and while Melville commends us, he at the same time condemns us for our faults. If we intend to follow Melville's advice, we should probably be content, as Father Mapple preaches, to "obey God" and "disobey ourselves", fervently hoping that our inherent evil will be overshadowed by goodness.

CRITICISM

While it is not too difficult for a student who has something to say to write a good essay on a fairly simple subject, it is extremely hard to combine profundity with clarity. The perfect merger of the two is, of course, the ultimate goal of every writer.

This essay, while certainly the most complex in content, is by no means the most lucid essay in this book. It deserves attention, however, because, while it is not altogether successful, its author has *nearly* succeeded in producing a remarkable piece of literary criticism.

The overall organization, the illustrations selected to support the author's thesis, and many of the rhetorical techniques employed, are excellent. The essay's major weaknesses are found in the author's development of individual points: Certain sentences do not communicate effectively because the author has not explained his ideas sufficiently.

The opening paragraph immediately focuses attention on the specific subject of the paper — the difficulty of discerning good from evil — rather than on the novel as a whole. The novel, then, is subordinated to a larger consideration; the essay as a whole deals with Melville's presentation of, and solution to, the philosophical question.

The introduction, however, is not totally effective, and its weaknesses are typical of those throughout the essay. The author writes that we "expect to find this separation of villain and hero, whether through characters or ideas". He means, of course, that we expect to find characters who are either all good or all bad, and that these are usually termed "hero" and "villain".

Errors of this type are often the result of attempting to say more in a sentence or phrase than is possible. One should aim at expressing ideas in as few words as possible, but never at the expense of clarity.

EXERCISES

1. Underline each sentence in the essay which does not communicate the author's meaning clearly to the reader. Determine from the context precisely what he meant to say, and then rewrite each sentence.

2. The second sentence of paragraph one does not provide a smooth transition between the opening of the paper and the author's first mention of *Moby Dick*. In addition to the weaknesses mentioned in the Criticism section, the sentence contains the totally unnecessary phrase "we of the modern western world". Rewrite sentences two and three.

3. Paragraph six deals with cannibalism. In what sense is Ahab's consuming of his own soul an example of this?

4. The author's final paragraph would be more effective if broken into two separate paragraphs. At what point should the break occur? Why? Would this require the shifting of any individual sentences? Would a transition be required?